The Angels Speak:
Secrets from
the Other Side

Conversations Along the Path

by
Jennifer Martin
and Rosemary Dean

Disclaimer

The information contained in *The Angels Speak: Secrets from the Other Side* is intended only for information. It is sold with the understanding that the publisher, editors, authors, and advisors are not engaged in rendering legal, accounting, or other professional services through this book.

While the publisher, editors, authors, and advisors have made every effort to ensure the accuracy of the information in *The Angels Speak: Secrets from the Other Side*, they assume no responsibility for either typographical or informational errors, inaccuracies, omissions of either people or places, or any other inconsistencies within the book. Any slights of people or organizations are totally unintentional. Any misuse or improper use of written material is totally unintentional.

Prairie Angel Press, the editors, authors, and advisors for *The Angels Speak: Secrets from the Other Side* have neither liability nor responsibility to any person or entity for loss or damage incurred, or allegedly incurred, directly or indirectly from the information contained in *The Angels Speak: Secrets from the Other Side*.

If you are unwilling to be bound by the above statement, you may return *The Angels Speak: Secrets from the Other Side* for a full refund.

Published by Prairie Angel Press
P.O. Box 340815
Sacramento, CA 95834-0815

Library of Congress Catalog Card Number: 95-69470

Dedication

To my protectors, Mary and Tony Martin, my parents, and Sarah, my guardian angel. Thanks for your enduring love and guidance.

—JM

For all those wounded people—those who have suffered and those who are finding the way.

—RD

Acknowledgements

This book could not have been created without the enthusiasm, expertise, and support of my husband and soul mate, Bud Gardner, Carol O'Hara, Susan Madden, Ric and Jody Hornor, Dan Poynter, and Rose Gasser. Special thanks to my son, Cael Kuhlman, my friends, and co-workers for their abiding interest and encouragement.

—JM

Many thanks to my husband, Richard Dean, long-suffering though he is, to those on the other side, and to all those whose belief in me has made it possible for me to grow.

—RD

Table of Contents

Preface

I remember the first time I met Rosie Dean in January of 1992. Summoned to my home to do a psychic reading, this roly-poly red-headed wonder walked into my living room, glanced at my parents' elopement picture on the mantel, and then innocently asked if I'd like to speak to my father. Now, I was absolutely delighted to speak again to my father, especially since he had died over a year before! The session that followed was the most incredible I had ever witnessed in my life. Not only could she tune in to my father, my cat, and my past lives, but she confirmed the contacts that I had had with my guardian angel, Sarah, whose warning saved me from being killed in a car accident in July of 1990. So, when my burning desire to learn about the angelic kingdom reached a gnawing, gut-wrenching hunger for knowledge, Rosie provided the perfect answer: She could channel information directly from the angels themselves.

I have related to angels all of my life. As a small child attending Catholic schools, I recited the same prayer every night:

Angel of God, my guardian dear, to whom God's love commits me here, ever this day be at my side, to light, to guard, to rule and guide.

Many times, I'd ask my guardian angel to help me on a test or wake me up at a certain time in the morning. On more than one occasion, I actually heard a choir of angels singing. So, when angels suddenly piqued the interest of the American public and *Time* magazine's December 1993 cover proclaimed the fact that nearly 70% of the American public believed in angels, I reveled in the angel books and artifacts which began glutting the market. I began angel-collecting like a shark in a feeding frenzy. I collected ceramic angels, angel mobiles, angel bumperstickers, angel cards, even angel earrings. If someone had invented angel cereal with little golden halos floating in your bowl, I would have bought it. And, of course, I read every angel book I could get my hands on. But, oddly enough, none of them satisfied my curiosity about the angelic kingdom. I wanted to know more. Just like the *National Enquirer*, my inquiring mind wanted to know! I wanted to know, for example, how angels experienced God. Did angels giggle or gossip with each other? How could they see each other if they didn't have bodies? And why would some angelic souls descend into dense human bodies to experience the human condition? These and a million other questions went unanswered until I decided to ask the angels themselves through the channeling of Rosie Dean.

We began meeting at my home in February of 1994. After visiting and talking about personal things, we'd begin tape recording. During these sessions, Rosie would go into an altered state and while the "Rosie Dean personality" floated somewhere, the angels would "hug" her, they said, and through some kind of telepathy use her body to deliver their replies to my questions.

At first, we heard from an angelic group, singularly named Isabelle, because Rosie could not deal with the fact that "Isabelle" was really a congregation of anywhere from 15 to more than 3,000 angels and former humans on the other side. It was far more comfortable for her to talk to Isabelle as if she were one person, even though on the tapes one might hear a booming male voice take over or a bit of an Irish brogue slip through. One visitor who joined us on two occasions, Gabriel the Archangel, flat-out intimidated Rosie because of his formality (he wouldn't let her call him "Gabe"). But his technique to cleanse our emotional hearts was so profound that we felt it was the Cartier diamond in a treasure trove of gems. And there were other fascinating folks like David from the 11th dimension of our earth; sweet Miriam, who lived during the time of Christ; and Safar, our eloquent friend from Persia, 350 B.C.

These entities had made a pact with Rosie that they could channel through her body if they'd agree to keep their message and vocabulary simple. When each session was over, the real Rosie would come back as if out of a deep sleep, unaware of any of the conversation that had just taken place. Sometimes, I'd play portions back to her for her reaction, but more often than not, I'd summarize the interesting highlights for her. Her reaction was totally unexpected. To most of it, she'd say, "Oh, I don't believe that," while to much of the rest, she'd stare into space with a glazed look and reply, "I don't understand that. What does that mean?" Once in a while she'd hear something profoundly touching and exclaim, "I never thought of it like that!" No matter what her response was, it was obvious that Rosie Dean (who thought Charlemagne was an African-American in Harlem) was clearly not the authentic being speaking to me.

Unlike Rosie's, my reaction was one of being totally awe-struck. The angels' overwhelming wealth of wisdom, the breadth of their understanding and the scope of their vision took my breath away. Not only did I satisfy my curiosity about the angelic kingdom, but I was let in on their version of the untimely deaths of Marilyn Monroe, Elvis Presley, John F. Kennedy and other prominent Americans. Eventually, we delved into earthly mysteries like the Pyramids and the Bermuda Triangle, and even unearthly ones, like the many extra-terrestrials currently on our planet who will be "coming out" soon. We talked about people in the news like Michael Jackson, John Candy, Oprah Winfrey, Donald Trump, Stephen Spielberg, Jeffrey Dahmer, O. J. Simpson, Jackie Kennedy Onassis—whoever popped up in the headlines on a given day. One of the most intriguing sessions was their disclosure of the side of Jesus Christ that had been intentionally left out of the Bible—his human aspects, including his bad temper and rebellious nature, the life he shared with Mary Magdalene and their three children, and the true account of the events that had unfolded during the original Easter week.

Over the months, we grappled with the many problems inherent in humanity, with our need to learn through negative and positive polarities, and with the massive changes that will soon be facing us as our institutions topple and are rebuilt. The angels revealed how they constantly help each and every one of us overcome our fears and sometimes triumph over the ever-present chaos all around us. Finally, we learned that humankind, if we learn to "allow," will not only survive the tumultuous times that are coming, but, ultimately, will be triumphant in reaching new multidimensional levels of thinking and living.

Please understand that these conversations are given to you as a gift to receive at whatever level you choose. As the *true authors*, the angels, have said: your perceptions are your truths. If anything in this book rings true for you, then it is *your* truth. But, if there are parts that you cannot perceive, then that is not your truth at this time. You can always return to the book another time, or you can pass it on to a friend. In any case, we want to assure you that these messages are not ours—Rosie's or mine. We simply served as catalysts to bring you what we believe is straight from the hearts and minds of the angelic kingdom. The tapes were edited in the interest of the clarity, continuity, and propriety. Enjoy!

—Jennifer Martin

The Angels Speak: Secrets from the Other Side

Chapter 1

The Nature of the Angelic Kingdom

There are over 500 million species in the universe and a few coming into being. We have interaction with all of them in different forms.

N early 70% of the American public believes in angels. Images of angels can be seen in every aspect of our culture, from popular song lyrics to guardian angel pins adorning lapels. We've learned about angels from poetry, the Bible, and countless other sources. But who, recently, has ever talked to an angel? What are they really like? How do they experience each other and, more importantly, how do they perceive us? What's their view of our past and what do they foresee in our future? These and many more questions were answered by the angels known collectively as "Isabelle."

Isabelle

The group singularly described as "Isabelle" fluctuated in number, anywhere from 15 to more than 3,000 beings, some of whom had always been angels, and some of whom had been human at one time. They had chosen Rosie to channel their information because they wanted to keep their message simple, appealing to everyday people who were either just beginning their spiritual paths or seeking to expand their understanding of the nature of the angelic kingdom.

Channeling

While Rosie has the ability to consciously channel, she wanted to be totally "out" when Isabelle came through. Thus, Rosie had no conscious memory of our conversations with the angels, a process they described as "hugging."

Jennifer: Exactly how do you transmit your communication to us?

Isabelle: Mental telepathy is what you call it. We call it merging of the minds, the senses, or the vibrations.

J: You don't seem to have any problems with the English language, so do you just picture a message? Is it beyond language?

I: When one is speaking through what you term "channel," there is a tendency for us to use what is at hand. It is as if we have the use of voice boxes, memories, and simulation with your language through this personality. It has nothing to do with what we are trying to get through.

You must understand that a great many channels have a lot more intelligence, education, and life experiences, and we can assimilate things of a more complicated nature through those souls. This one has chosen to work with those souls who are in the beginning stages of spiritual awareness. And so she has been given that opportunity to learn in that way. It is not a matter of education or of life experiences that is so very important to this one. It is a matter of simplicity, and so we work with her in that way.

Those of us who choose to work with those of a more intellectual nature need to find other areas and other souls that can accommodate them. They do have some trouble at times trying to put thought processes into this one in a simplified version. Some of our thought processes that she is translating confuse her at some point, and so we try very hard not to confuse the vehicle.

J: She mentioned one time that she felt she had two bodies when you are speaking through her, that she can actually feel the physical body, but there's another body that she feels. Can you explain that?

I: You all have more than one body. Many of you think that what you see is what you get, that the human body is all that there is. But there are hundreds of aspects of your one human body, and there could be hundreds of bodies incorporated in one body. And this is what she is speaking of. Basically, she is defining the main body and the body immediately behind the main body. You call it etheric body. And this is what she is experiencing, but basically there are many, many aspects to your so-called solid body.

Sparks from God

Angels are the thought processes of the Light or Force we call God. These angelic forces are a continuous stream of thoughts coming into being and sent forth by God, like sparks flying out of a great bonfire.

I: We are the thought processes of your Light, of your Force, of your Source, of your God. And it is an interesting thing that so many humans do not think of your God as being a thinker, but indeed it is so. And every time a thought process came about, a light being came about, also. And where there was darkness, there is much light. We might tell you also that there is a continuous stream of thought processes coming into being in what you would call the angelic forces.

J: I'm assuming that since angels are continuous thoughts, they don't die.

I: They do not. As they have always been, as your Creator has always been, so they shall always be. There will never be a time in the history of mankind or any other planet or any other species for that matter, where we will not always be.

Energy Forms—Without Wings

Sparks from the Light that we call God, angels are forces who have come to promote and help different species. While we envision them as humans with wings, they are neither human nor do they have wings.

J: If we were looking at angels, not with human eyes, but as an angel would, looking upon another angel, what would we see?

I: You would see a light, and if you were very adept at it, as angels can be, you would see variations of color in that light, but if you happened to be on another planet, let us say the Pleiadians, you would take that thought process, and you would form it into the likeness of them. We are very adaptable.

J: If there are no wings, what is it that we see when we humans see the form of an angel?

I: You must understand that in terms of angels, it is very much the same in terms of humanness. Is it not true that some of you have greater abilities than others? Some of you are taller than others. You have different aspects of yourself that glow further out than others; is this not so? And it is the same with our species.

Some of us have been doing this for eons of time. Actually, we do not have time on this side. We go by your description. But there are some of us who are so very old and so very evolved that we form different vibrational frequencies. And so we take on the appearance of wings as a way of dispersing energy. It takes a great amount of energy to be an angel, just as it takes a great amount of energy to be human. If you did not have energy, you would not be human. You would be on our side. It's the same with angels. The more you evolve, the more energy you have, the more you have to disperse. And so the aspect of wings is what you see, and that is how you identify it. But we do not have feathers.

J: What is an angel's home like on the other side? How do angels co-exist with one another? What's their life like?

I: Say you were to have a room with many spotlights of different colors, hues, and vibrational levels, some a little cooler than others. You have a 40-watt bulb, a 60-watt bulb, and a 100-watt bulb, that would be something of what it's like, a warm blending feeling. It is a feeling of great comfort that there are so many souls who are blending into the greater whole.

J: So how do you see each other?

I: We identify each and every one by tones of colors. You see, colors have tone, did you know that? Each and every one has its own musical quality, let us say that. And we do identify that. We also identify by kinship. If you see a shade of beautiful pink circling around another shade of a little pinker, circling around another shade of light pink, circling around another shade of medium pink, and so on and so on, those are the souls who work in service for the same thing.

J: That's what you mean by kinship. So the colors change according to their role?

I: According to what the soul is needing to function as. And also like we said, each and every—let us say the word color, because that is the only way you'll understand—each and every color dances to its own vibrational sound. You have a wonderful instrument on your plane and you use it with music a great deal. It is something that makes color dance. We do not know what it is, but we have watched it and been fascinated. You have them in your home a great deal. The colors react to the sound of your music. It is a box.

J: And when they hear a new sound, a different light comes on?

I: Yes. That is very much like we are. We vibrate to different tone levels. You all do. But we do here as a way of recognition, and those who are of like tone and like color vibrate and dance to the same philosophy.

Angelic Powers

The range of angelic powers is all-encompassing and awesome.

I: Angels have the ability to do as much as what you would call your God. They have an ability to destroy. They have an ability to create, to evolve, to offer solace, and to create miracles. They are the minions of your Light and are put into force in place of what you term God.

J: As angels evolve, as they learn new things, how do they find out about each other?

I: As we have always been, we have always known of each other. And the way we evolve is by service. We do not evolve by reading books, or seeing great plays. We evolve by the energy that we expend on other species, other planes. We must tell you also that every human has had the opportunity to be an angel.

J: How is that?

I: Because at one point, as you are created by a thought process, you are light, are you not? An energy form.

J: The soul?

I: Indeed. And do you not have a choice as to what that soul is to do? Some of us choose not to be in human form. Some of us choose not to be in *any* form, other than an energy form. But those souls that were created by a thought process have always got the choice to do as they wish to do and to evolve in the way they wish to evolve. That is why there are some forms of angels who have come to you in human form, have become human so to speak. They have made the choice to help out this species in any way they can.

Let us tell you a secret. There is always a choice, and those of you who choose to work with your light in human form, or for that matter in any species' form will always have the choice of choosing to work with your light as a human, as any other number of species, or as an angel.

He? She? Fido?

There are millions of angels who intervene for us when we call out for help. Although they have appeared to us as females or males, there really is no gender in their kingdom. They just create bodies which will get them the fastest recognition so that they can begin the task of helping us out.

I: It is interesting that we can appear as a dog, and you would not think so much of that species or of that angelic form as a help to you. We could, however, appear as a very stern male figure, and that for some would be a great help, and they would put their faith in that soul. Just as you insist on naming your Creator as a He or She or Mother, Father, Son...all those things. It is neither. But we give you what you need, or what you ask for on a higher level.

The universe is like a hologram in the mind of God, and it tends to match with our picture of reality. In the same way, the angels tend to comply with what we wish to experience as reality and, at this time, that means angelic beings who are wise, loving guides, rescuers, and seers.

Angel Assignments

Angelic souls often take on human form so that they can be uplifting role models and advance humanity along a more spiritual path. Miriam, one of the Isabelle group who spent one of her lives in the time of Jesus Christ, explained how angels take on human form.

M: It is a change in vibrations or frequencies, you see. We ask you, do you see radio frequencies?

J: No, but we know they exist.

M: Then how can you change a channel? Do you know what it is that changes the frequencies?

J: What? The dial. You just tune to a different frequency.

M: But, is that all that is required, to have a dial? If so, could you not have a dial in your hand and use it in there?

J: Well, you need a receiver and all the equipment to do that.

M: Indeed so. And that's exactly what happens to us. We have to have receivers. We have to have energy that is given to us on a higher plane. When angels choose to go into any form, it needs to be okayed.

J: From another source?

M: From *the* Source. And when it is validated and there is reason for it, then we are allowed to use the power of the Creator which we will say to you is like electricity that is very high and very powerful. And we take some of that energy, and we are able to transform. Another time, if many of us get together and wish to speak to and help other souls on your planet, we first ask permission and then we get together. Then we have a conductor, and we all put our energy to the conductor and it becomes so.

J: Now can the process be reversed? Can humans take on angelic form? Can they become angels?

M: Indeed they can.

J: And how do they do that?

M: Where they first started out that way.

J: So they were originally angels.

M: Indeed.

J: And then they took on human form and they decided to return back to angelic form.

M: Indeed. And we say to you something interesting. When you choose to come into human form from the angelic field, you go to a lower level. And if you choose to stay on our side and to come back into the form that you call angelic, you need to come up a few levels in order to do so, and that requires a great deal of healing, of learning, and of being of service. You cannot come back to where you first began because when you become human, we shall say this as nice as possibly, you become solid in your thinking and, uh...

J: Denser.

M: Indeed. In many different ways. And so if you choose to become angelic in form again, it takes a great deal of thinking on this aspect, and you must show that you wish to do so, and it might take at least 500 of your years to do so, if not a thousand.

J: Well, I know I want to return back to angelic form.

M: But, you see, you are not human, so you do not have to do that which is required.

J: Oh, I don't have to go through the 500 to 1000 year-trial?

M: Indeed, you do not.

J: Oh, that's good.

M: What is not good about this is you must keep coming back to be of service. Now again, we say, my friend, that it is not Jennifer who is angelic. It is the soul of Jennifer who is angelic.

J: Oh, I'm sure people will tell you that Jennifer is certainly not angelic. (laughs)

M: But then again you must understand that you came to learn humanness so that you can identify with humans. If you did not learn humanness, you certainly would not identify.

In American history, two notable angels who took human form were Abraham Lincoln and Benjamin Franklin. While both were dedicated to promoting humanitarian efforts, neither one knew consciously that he was an angel—each just had an inkling that he was "good."

Today we have a modern day angel in talk show host Oprah Winfrey.

I: That is, indeed, a very old soul. She is a grand soul in the scheme of things. She has come to serve many, my friend. She has learned much in the lessons of negativity, so she can reach out to millions of souls who have gone through similar treatment. She is part of what we call the light force.

J: Yes. You can see that by the issues Oprah brings up, the way she deals with people, the love that she has. The compassion comes through. She is truly a light worker. I recognized her as one.

I: Immediately. For you are one, also. Of like mind.

As part of their assignment to protect us, angels often interact with animals to help us. Sometimes when a dog saves a child from drowning, it's the result of an angel helping an animal to go beyond itself. Besides giving guidance to animals, some angels are responsible for guiding plant life, trees, and flowers. So much for turgor pressure!

I: Have you ever seen a wildflower growing up through a cement street? Do you think that it is rather remarkable that something could do this? And what do you feel about that little flower which has such perseverance? Does it not enlighten you? Does it not make your heart soar for that little plant to be so strong-willed? Does it not make you feel good about creation? Do you really think that that plant did not have guidance and protection?

It was there for a purpose, my friend. You have a little plant to make you think on a higher level. So there is a purpose for that plant for human beings, and there is guidance for that plant.

J: So really they are metaphors. There's a lesson to be learned in just looking at the world and really observing.

I: Indeed, there is. There is nothing that is wasted.

J: There are no accidents.

I: And there are no unplanned lessons. Everything is put to use, everything, my friend. We have no garbage on our side.

J: (laughs) That's great.

Caution: Angels at Play

Just as they do with us, angels interact with each other, although in doing so, they do not experience the same emotions that we do.

J: Do angels play? Do they gossip? Do they ever get mad at each other?

I: We do not have a great deal of emotion on this side as you know it. But, yes, we play. We have great joy. That is one of the basic emotions that we do have. But we do not have emotion as you know it. Again, let us ask you how it feels to have your heart soar. If you could multiply that feeling a hundred thousand times, that is what we would describe as our joy. We do have sadness at times when we have not been able to complete a project. There is a great deal of sadness when one of our projects or one of our cares chooses to let go and not complete his or her project, his or her experience; then there is a feeling of sadness. It is different in that it is not a sadness that says we have failed. It is a sadness that this one will have to experience again.

But we do play. We do have what you call vacation days where we are free and we enjoy all. But gossip? We do have that in a different way. We do say to another, someone who is close to us, "Look at what my little one has accomplished. You see? This soul is so light. There is so much goodness-soul." And we are proud of our charges. It is as if, "Oh, look at the God in this one." We are proud to be connected. And you could term that gossip.

J: You kind of share all that fun together.

I: Indeed. That is something that all species do no matter what species it is. In any part of your universe it is the one common factor among all species, all souls, that we share. And most the time, it is that we share our joy.

Time as They Know It

One of the most difficult concepts to grasp is the angelic perspective of time.

I: What you call the Source or the Creator was the whole. Everything that has ever been, ever shall be, is all wrapped up into one gigantic being of force, light, vibration. And so it is hard to explain that when things began, they already were.

J: It's hard to us to comprehend that since we're so locked into linear time.

I: And that is the problem with your earth plane at this time. Most of you need to have explanations that are finite in your thinking. It's as if you have a brick wall, and you cannot go past that brick wall. And that brick wall that you call time holds a great deal of consternation for many of you.

But what has ever been in the mind of the Creator has always been. And so it came into being, and it continues. Everything that has ever been done, that has ever been thought of, that has ever been planned has already been in effect in that giant vibration or light force that you call Creator. We will simplify. What has always been will always be. What is the present and the past and the future is all one. There is no time period in our environment or sphere.

Understand that all is one, that the past, the present and the future is happening all at one point in your history; there is no past, present or future. It is all happening at once.

It is confusing in that we do not understand your time, either. We do not understand why you need to put labels and periods upon your history. Your history is always expanding. It never ceases until you flow back to the Creator. But it is happening all at once. Let us ask you a question. Do you realize that most stars that you are seeing in the present time have already died?

J: Yes. Thousands of years ago.

I: How can this be if it is the present?

J: Well, we're seeing the light from the stars because the light travels at a certain speed.

I: But, most of you choose to think these things are very solid indeed. And so, if you were to say to a person in Kenya, that that beautiful star you are seeing, that light isn't really there any more, do you think that person would believe you?

J: (laughs) No.

I: But look, I see it. It has to be there. You understand? And so we say to you that *all* is illusion.

Let us say to you, if you have a mirror, and you look at yourself, and you see yourself in the mirror, and in that mirror again you see yourself, and in that mirror again you see yourself, is that all not happening at once?

And yet that is how your lives are. Things change, indeed, but it is all happening at the same time.

J: It's just that in this planet things appear to us sequentially.

I: In this planet, you also think in terms of the word "finitely." But, that is not true, either.

J: It's infinite.

I: Indeed.

J: Is there a difference in terminology between infinite and eternal?

I: Indeed, there is. When you are dealing in the infinite, you are dealing in expansion. When you are dealing in eternity, you are dealing in finality. It is a time period.

There are some souls who choose to go on infinitely. They will not ever get enough of learning, enough of expansion. There are some souls who already have had enough and choose to go back to the beginning.

That is another interesting thing. Do you believe that your God created the beginning? Do you believe that you came from the head of the Creator, let us say, as a spark? Then how can you go back to the beginning if that has already happened? You see, it's just words.

J: You're right. It's mind-boggling.

I: Indeed, it is. Much more than you can ever imagine. But we try to simplify those things. We get greatly confused by your time, also. There are other souls on other planets who are greatly confused by your time.

J: Do they experience the same sense of time on other planets? Are there other species who have this kind of perception?

I: Some do, but some don't. There are many creatures who are observing your planet who have come from many light years away, but have different ways of incorporating time and expansion, so they may travel a great deal faster than you can ever imagine. It is very complicated for them to understand that you move so slowly.

J: I can imagine that.

I: And so it is a completely confusing idea, but we say to you it all just is. It is all now. We do not say that is the present. We say that it is all just now. And again, it is expansion.

The Creator

In thinking about the vast powers of the angels, it was only natural to wonder if they played a part in our creation.

I: There are a great many theories, are there not, that you as well as we are co-creators. We must tell you at the very beginning of this entire process that energy which you call God was the one, the only, and everything else was combined to make the whole. You see, it was not that you had one person who became lonely and that person needed company.

J: The Adam and Eve story.

I: Yes. It is that what you call the Source or the Creator was the whole. That everything that has ever been, ever shall be, is all wrapped up into one gigantic being of force, light, vibration. And so it is hard to explain that when things began, they already were.

J: Can you tell us how you experience the Creator? What qualities of God do you experience?

I: Think of some light that is so immense and so bright and so warm that even with the strongest feelings that you can come to with that thought process, you still could not experience the immensity and the warmth of the Light we see. Let us ask you a question. Have you ever been out in the cold and your whole body was frozen? And then you came into a cheery room where there was nothing but brightness and warmth and you slowly began to thaw out and there was a point when everything was right with your world. That is the feeling multiplied approximately one million times. Now, how do we explain that to you, but that everything is right as it should be, everything is on line as it should be, everything is taken care of as it should be, you understand?

J: Yes, I do. That's because I'm relating it to an out-of-the-body experience I once had and that feeling of total connection, total ease. I felt so peaceful. There's no other explanation. You can't describe it.

I: *Would you like to know a secret?* The closest that you will ever come on your earth plane to this immensity, this beautiful feeling, this brightness and warmth, is when you die.

It is a total acceptance. At that very moment that life leaves the body is when you feel acceptance with yourself, your Creator, your earth, and your sphere. And that is about as close as you can come to the feeling of being in the Creator's presence.

J: What is your name for God?

I: We do not have a name for God. We have what you would consider a tone. Think of the clearest, highest-sounding tinkle of a bell that you can think of. It is very hard to describe because you have nothing like it in your world. But if you heard a pleasing bell on the wind, something that is very high and very faint, it would be somewhat like that.

At one time the Old Testament portrayed God as a terrible being of thunder and light, and if we crossed that deity, we were bound to roast in hell fire. But when humankind reached a new understanding of love and gentleness, the image of God changed in our Bible.

Why is that so? Do you really think that the image of God changed for your benefit? Or is it that it is always changing because you were always changing? When you take a child and you explain your Jesus or Buddha or any of the other deities to that child, do you explain it in adult terms? No, you would explain it to a child, do you not?

And so the information that comes to you is on a par with your growth. And this is what is happening at this time. More and more of you are beginning to understand on a higher level what it's all about, so we give you more and more. We comply with the growth.

In the beginning of your creation, things indeed were very simple because you dealt with the earth, with survival, feeding, clothing and very little else. And so you needed a God who was stronger and fiery. Someone who was all strength. As you grew to love each other and to reach out and expand your own energies, then the God as you know It, reached out and expanded that energy. And you are going again, once again into a simplification of energies. But in this time period, instead of having a terrible, fiery deity, you will have a loving God, someone who allows, someone whom you call father-figure or mother-figure. And that is what is needed at this time. It is a positive growth.

We might tell you another secret. Your God tends to enjoy the experience that He or She or It has created, whatever you choose to say.

J: So does It experience those things through us?

I: Indeed, It does. You see, the Source as you know It experiences the whole, experiences all, but It is an on-going thing, has never had a beginning or an ending or a middle, for that matter.

J: If God experiences everything through us, why would God choose to experience pain and suffering?

I: Why not?

J: Why not? Because it hurts.

I: Does it hurt you?

J: Pain and suffering? You bet.

I: Why do you think that it would hurt God?

J: Well, if God experiences through us, wouldn't God have that feeling of...

I: You must understand something. Your Light, your God, does not experience feelings as you do.

J: So when we go through pain and suffering, what does God feel then?

I: Let us say knowledge. If you could put your feelings into knowledge, it is assimilated in that order. It would be somewhat like your God experiences.

J: So, God doesn't feel our emotions, just gets the message.

I: Last time we looked, we did not see a body of any kind.

J: So there are no feelings as we know them?

I: Just love as you know it.

J: What do you experience?

I: We experience the very same. It is very hard to explain because our feelings, our emotions, are not the same. As we do not have bodies, we do not feel pain on your level. But, we feel sadness of the whole. It is as if the light of ourselves becomes a bit dimmer when we have a charge who experiences pain and sadness. It is as if the energy is not as bright. It's a different feeling altogether. Do you have a little switch that you could turn your light down? That is how we would explain what we are speaking of. It is a sadness because the light dims. It is not a physical pain, a physical emotion. It's that our light dims for another.

The Angelic Hierarchy

The more involved an angel is, the more specialized it is as well. There are some, like the archangels, who are favored very highly by God and specialize in overseeing certain segments of history and various populations in species.

Traditionally, the angelic kingdom has been divided into nine levels of angels, among them the cherubim and seraphim, angels which we depict as little children, but who are the very highest angelic forms of all.

I: Cherubim and seraphim have no need to have a field or specialty. They have no need to deal with anything but love.

J: Oh, so we symbolize them as babies because of their innocence and closeness to the Creator.

I: Yes, indeed. And the interesting thing about this all is that, in truth, is what *you* have to do. When you have experienced the all, when you have experienced the whole and there is no need to experience any more, you go back to the beginning.

J: It's what Teilhard de Chardin, the Jesuit philosopher, said about going from Alpha to Omega. That's all there is.

I: Indeed. But just as in your world there are teachers and doctors who choose to specialize in certain areas or fields, that is the same as our plane. You consider them archangels. They choose to specialize. And they do move at a higher, faster vibration, and it is because they have learned and experienced a great deal more than others.

It's not like we have progression like grades. It is that we have accumulated more energy. Just as we were explaining to you that the energy makes one expand, that is what we are speaking of with the archangels, that because they have experienced more, and they have put more energy into their vibrations; they have expanded, and that is the vibrational level.

Fallen Angels

Like the Creator, angels not only have the ability to evolve, but they can offer solace, create miracles, and even bring destruction.

Even though angels do not experience linear time in their kingdom as we do here, they have been a part of our history, and have been immortalized in all human forms of communication, from books and plays to songs and videos. The Bible has been the main source of the drama involving Lucifer's ousting from heaven, along with the other fallen angels.

The angelic rendition of the fallen angel story, however, differs substantially from most traditional religions. According to Isabelle, the angels were simply complying with our crying need for a destructive force to be manifested in the world as a way for us to understand the concepts of positive and negative.

For example, think about learning the concept of "temperature." Most of the time we learn it through comparison and contrast. If we understand hot and cold and all the degrees in between, we can generally assume that we grasp the concept of temperature. And that's how we learn many things in life. We categorize them as good or bad, positive or negative.

Because of our need to understand the concepts of good and evil, the "fallen" angels participated in the heaven and hell saga. The great Biblical drama, starring Lucifer as the antagonist and the Archangel Michael as the hero, provided us a way to understand positive/negative duality which, when you think about it, is the nature of the universe.

I: Throughout your time, there has been a need for good and bad as a way to explain why some of you have to go through so much trial, so much pain and sorrow. And so at the beginning, there was a great need to explain this away and so we complied. But in the angelic world, there is no good or bad. It is just so. What is needed will be given. Whatever energy that is needed to be supplied to those who are learning will be given.

And so your demons and your Satan, all those souls, come into being because of a great need for the negative. As a human being, how would you ever know what the good, positive experiences were if you never experienced anything but? And when you go through a negative experience, don't you feel like you have grown when you have conquered that experience? That you have had much spiritual growth?

Angel Reception (Adjust Your Antennas)

Throughout history, people like Thomas Aquinas, Rudolph Steiner, Dante and Milton have written about angels. Some of them learned about the angelic kingdom from childhood, mythology, and religion. Others heard voices. Some had dreams. Because a scholar like Aquinas preferred to receive information about them strictly on an intellectual level, the angels complied and relayed cerebral messages to him.

Given Rosie's basic nature and preference, however, they have given information to her on the heart level because that is where she is most comfortable receiving it. It doesn't matter at which level it is received, though, because the angelic message will get through if we choose to allow it.

Guardians will appear to us if we want them to, but many of us would be traumatized by their appearance.

J: Because I'd probably be a bit jittery seeing her in all her magnificent light, I've asked Sarah, my guardian angel, to appear to me as a bird now and then, as a visible reminder that she is around. And does she! Sometimes when I'm driving I see birds whose swooping is in perfect sync with the movement of my car. I've even been startled to see a bird flying at window level perpendicular to my car while I was driving on the freeway!

I: Humans need to see substance, as any other species needs to see substance. You know, there are many many earth planes, and there are many different species in one dimension or another, and they all seem to need that type of substance. They need to have help from those like them. And so we willingly create bodies, substance that will get us to the fastest possible recognition so that we can begin the task of helping out.

Guardian Angels

Guardian angels are assigned to each and every one of us, from before we take our first breath, until they pull us over on their side as we take our last. They help us plan out our lives before we are born, and they are there to welcome us back when we return home.

I: An angel can be human at one time and guardian the next. It is usually a group of souls that come together. Let us say the group with this one is 350 souls, and one chooses to be her guardian. It is a fallacy to say that we have always been together. Guardians to not always stay with the same soul.

J: During the same lifetime?

I: During the same lifetime, they stay. But there are times when you need a different type of guardian. For instance, this one (Rosie) has an issue with females, so her guardian is male, and she feels safe and comfortable with that.

J: Do all human beings have guardian angels?

I: Everyone has a guardian. *We will tell you another secret.* Even the guardian angels have guardian angels.

J: What do they need to be guarded for?

I: Let us ask you a question. Do you consider a guardian angel someone who just guards over you?

J: Well, that's part of it.

I: That's part of it, but it is also a bonding, a teaching, a togetherness, you know, a blending. It is a little bit of this path and the other path; you call it "this world" and "the other world." It is a blending of those two worlds. It is not the only thing for a guardian angel to do but protect. They do that, you must understand this, but it is also a bit of home away from home. And so we have guardians for those who are guardians for others, and we come into being when there is a great need.

We need to tell you that we have a home, just as you do. Angels have a home, but when they are in service, they are not at home. They are on different levels and planes, and they deal with those at a lower level. And so for us, too, there is a tendency to be homesick at times.

J: And so you need the camaraderie of the other angels, to go back and feel rejuvenated.

I: Indeed. And when we say that guardian angels have guardians also, we are speaking of that. At times they need to have a vacation and blend with those of a higher level.

J: Do guardian angels communicate with other people's guardians on their behalf?

I: All the time. Have you not ever asked for intervention with a child of yours? Do you think that it is always God? You must understand something. Your God lets everything happen freely. And when you're asking for intervention, you're usually asking for one of us to intercede for you, and a great deal of the time, it is your guardian angel who is doing so. And they may go to your child's angel to have a blending, and to ask that they be of service to this personality because the other is afraid.

J: Rosie had a question today from a friend of hers. If a child has a guardian angel, how can bad things happen to the child? I think this woman lost a child, so she was wondering why that child wasn't protected.

I: First of all, we will tell you that all souls, including those of your animal world, plant world, and even your earth, have guardian angels. We see to it that this little soul is given what is needed, and we see how it has chosen to participate in some sort of lesson for others.

When a child passes over, we do not see that this is a bad thing. There is nothing wasted, my friend. Not a soul. Not a life. Not even if it is only but one moment.

In your terminology, protection means something totally different than it does to us. You see, you think in terms of bad and good, and protection is from the bad, is it not? In our terminology, protection means that we allow whatever the soul comes in to do, and we try to help that. And that is protection, or guarding, so that those souls tend to come in and do what they must do.

Basically, those who are of the angelic force who have never become human or any other species tend to be very mystified at the idea of your death. We say to you, do you not go to work every morning? Do you not come home? That is our idea of our plane. You go to work, you learn, and then you come home. And it has nothing to do with what you think of as good and bad. It has to do with completing the purpose and the project.

So, when you honor those little souls that have come, have done their work, and you celebrate that moment that they were here, then your whole process will change in the idea of death.

J: Yes. It'll be a celebration of their life, not remorse over their leaving.

Sometimes when a situation calls for a great expansion of energy, our guardian's guardians come to the rescue and provide added force. There are times when we are experiencing difficulties that require the intervention of other teachers or guides who are specialists. For example, if we are having problems managing money and pray for some relief, our guardian angels might enlist the help of other angelic beings who have chosen to become experts in finance. Then again, there are those souls who rushed back to earth without much of a plan and require even more assistance.

I: That personality's guardian angel and this personality's guardian angel get together and help plan, when the other one has not chosen to have a blueprint. If their charges need help, then there will be those who choose to deal with their charge.

They Never Leave Us

It's important to understand that even during traumatic episodes of rape or murder, our guardians are still with us. Because it may be an individual's purposeful choice, the angels do not stop these tragedies. But they do what they can to love and help the soul through that painful episode.

I: We are trying to console and to wrap our arms around them while this is happening. And that is what some of you call "shock." It is when your essence is much closer to ours than you can know. It is a blending of that essence, so it makes some of those episodes that you call traumatic or violent a little less frightening for the soul because they are not totally in the body. And that is our gift to you. We have made a decision eons ago not to interfere in a purpose, in a challenge, in an experience, basically because it is not our right to walk your path. We can warn. We can say to you, "Watch out!" And if you choose to listen, that is all and good, but if you choose not to, we cannot say to you, "That was a mistake."

We can put our arms around you, what you call arms, and we can love, and we can send gentle vibrations to the mind and to the heart as a way of you blending, and so that you do not always feel what is happening to your body. We do as much as possible, but some of you choose to have very trying experiences. And we tell you that it also touches us. When you are putting your arms around a soul who is in great trauma, you feel the emotion and it is not pleasant to us. That is because we are coming to the lower plane, and that is because the emotions are bombarding our energy.

J: So, it's hurtful to you?

I: It can be very painful, yes, or sad.

J: Sad. I was thinking of my godson who died in a car accident when he was 19, and the driver fell asleep at the wheel. She was not injured seriously, but his skull was crushed and he died. I was devastated when I was told that he was awake when it happened. I have always hoped that the angels would have protected him so that he wouldn't have felt any pain when he went out.

I: You have to understand that they did so and that this soul was in shock. He was not in the body.

J: Oh, good. I'm glad.

I: Many souls, and you can ask almost any one who chooses to have a near-death experience, are quite astounded that what they consider to be great pain was not there. That it became quiet, loving, warm, and light.

And so we do our best. Whenever you choose to have an experience like this, we try very hard to make it as least traumatic as possible, and we do help you out of the body, my friend. In fact, we even at times help pull.

So the human being does not experience as much as you think. This is why many of us are confused at why so many have so much fear of dying. You see, we try to make it the least traumatic as possible, and that is why you have human beings who are terminal and tend to become very serene towards their death because they are not all in the body and are experiencing warmth, joy, and love.

J: Yes. Some of them actually have smiles on their faces.

I: We would say 90% of those who choose to die in that way have done so.

J: So they have their angels around them and they're receiving love.

I: And warmth and light and joy. And at the beginning as we put our energy toward you and encircle you, we experience fear, anger and pain. And it is not something that we choose to do on our own. We choose to do this as a way of learning and a way of growing ourselves. But it is not very pleasant, and we do not wish to deal with it most of the time.

J: Right. Well, it doesn't last too long, though.

I: A second or so. Again, we say to you, even as your Creator experiences through human beings and other entities, so do we, and you understand it is not a thinking process, but it is an experiencing of emotion that we experience, and so we learn from it.

And what we learn is to give unconditional love at a moment when there is so much fear. We learn from it, and we grow from it. But it is not something we think about. It is something we just do.

No Peeking Please

It's rather unnerving, when you think about it, to realize that your guardian angel never leaves you, especially when you'd like some privacy during showers or intimate encounters. But then again, we're only colored lights to them.

I: You have to understand that those who are seeking privacy put up their own wall. But it does not mean that the angel is not there next to the wall or to the door. They're saying, "If you need me, I will be here."

But again, we must tell you something very funny. Angels, souls of any kind, do not see you as a human being.

—34—

They do not see you functioning as a human being. They see the color changes. It is as if you are a giant kaleidoscope. And the colors are constantly changing. This is what we see.

J: So you just notice more change in the color.

I: Indeed.

J: Well, what colors denote certain emotions or actions?

I: When one is at prayer, we see the most beautiful purples and blues. When one is going through a rough time and beginning to heal from that emotional time, we see pinks and greens.

When one is feeling quite badly in health, there are many gray areas and yellows, kind of a dull yellow, and indeed, human beings tend to have many colors at once, and there may be some duller and some brighter which denotes where the problem is. When one is having, your word, "privacy," and being human, there is a great deal of red and orange. And what we do is play with our wings for a while.

Angels Among Us

Angels are always beside us, and we could see them if we choose to. Sometimes it's too scary for us to even think about seeing them. Often it's easier just to sense their presence or hear their voices.

I remember back in June of 1990 when my guardian angel warned me of an impending disaster by shouting in my left ear: "You are going to be in a car accident." For two weeks after that, I was excruciatingly careful every time I got into my car, knowing that if I were fated to be in an accident, I would not be the cause of it.

On July 1st, I was going to be an extra in a movie being shot in San Francisco, so I went to Sonora to visit my friend, Diane, who had a large closet stuffed with period clothes. I picked out some 1960s outfits, and she rolled my hair in curlers to create the '60s look. Back in my car, I rolled down the windows to dry my hair and headed off for the city, stopping only at a fast foods restaurant to get an iced tea. As I reached for the tea, I remembered the warning and buckled both the shoulder and seat belts. This action saved my life because less than an hour later I was deliberately run off the road, my car flipping totally over and landing upright in the only spot in the area without trees. Because I had had the windows rolled down, no glass flew in to hurt me. And because I had both belts on, I didn't go through the windshield, and the car did not land on me.

When I reflect on that "accident," (there really are no such things) I realize that it symbolized being in "the fast lane" and becoming reckless in my relationships. I was being warned that my choices at the time would only lead to greater personal calamity. I know now that my guardian angel saved both my physical and spiritual life. The accident became a turning point for me to begin to create a more balanced life by healing old childhood wounds and stepping onto a more spiritual path which would allow me to manifest the higher aspects of my true self. But in telling others about hearing my angel's warning, I often find myself peering into skeptical, sometimes reproachful, faces. It's just too unbelievable for some.

I: So many of you ask to see your guardians, your angels and guides, but you are so afraid to see. If you were to see us, you would either not believe it, or would be frightened that there was something wrong with your minds.

J: But it doesn't have to be like that.

I: No, it doesn't. When human beings stop fearing those very things we're speaking of, then we will make much more progress.

J: Will that happen?

I: It is happening even now. Let us ask you. When you heard your guardian tell you about the accident, were you relieved or were you frightened?

J: I was glad for the warning because she saved my life

I: Yes, and isn't that something that we are supposed to do? But if she came to you one fair night and said to you, "Jennifer, let's go out and dance under the moon," would you tend to be as easy with that as you would a warning?

J: (laughs) Not quite as easy, I'm sure. But I would love to dance with my angel under the moon.

I: Then do so. As you know, she is always with you, and we say this to you truthfully that you do know. Then you must also know that you can dance under the moon with your guardian.

Even species in the animal and plant kingdoms are very aware of angels, but just accept that as a natural part of the environment.

I: Let's take the animal kingdom, if you will. Animals are much more progressive in their thinking. For them, things are true. They are just there. They do not question the energy of angels. They do not question the thought process of themselves. They do not question help. It is just there. And so we abide with those other kingdoms in a more natural way than we do with humans. That is why most of your animals see energy forms that you do not see. For them it is not a matter of positive or negative. It is not a matter of do I or don't I. It is a matter of, there is something there...do I need to be cautious? It is an instinct, and animals do not make judgments except for survival.

Angels Among Others

Besides all the species on earth, angels interact with species on other planets as well, appearing to them in an acceptable form.

J: Do angels have interaction with other beings? For example, you mentioned the Pleiadians.

I: There are over 500 million species in the universe and a few coming into being. We have interaction with all of them in different forms.

J: Can you tell us about that?

I: Again, we say to you that we comply with our appearance. But there are some planets, some planes that exist with our plane side by side and know we are there, but really have no interest. It is just a fact of life, much like your animals. There is no questioning. We just are. We are there to comply with the energies that are needed.

J: But do you act in the same way, helping them out, as you do with us?

I: Indeed, we do not. We comply with what is ever needed. They allow energy when it is there, and they do not have a great expectation of anything new or unusual or exciting. It is just common place.

Angel Energy

We are coming to a point of transformation in our lives on earth where, like the angels, we will embrace the concept of learning through love and not polarity. The more we are drawn to the idea of love on a higher level, the more we will come to the idea of non-polarity.

I: *We will tell one other secret.* That is why so much of our energy is being pushed into your world at this time. It has no polarity at all. You may take of that energy and use it for whatever you wish. It is all around you. It's there for the using. Have you been in your house one fine morning and felt in love with the world? How does the air feel to you?

J: Light.

I: Indeed. And when other people come into the room that you're in, how do you think they feel?

J: Joyful.

I: Indeed. And that is how it is used. You manifest that which you desire and it happens. It is a chance to learn that there does not need to be negative and positive in your world.

Chapter 2

The Human Re-Condition

Love is the most powerful emotion of mankind, and they are always afraid that they will not be worthy of it.

Why Now?

While angels have always been with us on earth, they have not always been as strongly felt as they are now. They are blending their presence into our existence more now than ever before because of the great need for human beings to take a quantum leap in consciousness and become the multidimensional beings that we are intended to be.

I: So many of you are ready to grow into mighty energy forces on your own, and when you begin to open up to that energy and to all that you can create and all that has been created for you, then you begin to see with different aspects those higher energy levels.

And there are so many of you at this time who are choosing to deal with the positive aspects of energy rather than the negative, so we allow you to see the positive aspects of angels.

It is your growth, my dear, not ours. We have been waiting for a very long time for you to all come to this understanding. We would say about one-third of your earth population is coming to this at this time.

And when the energies are promoted in this way, and so many of you are putting your energies towards us, we begin to put more of our energies towards you, and so the levels of frequencies come closer together. As you reach, so do we. And then we can all begin to work at a faster pace.

Getting to the Heart of the Matter

One result of this leap in consciousness relates to the development of the emotional aspects of our personalities, specifically the expansion of our hearts.

I: *Let us tell you a secret.* Let's say fifty of your years ago, your humanness was on an intellectual level, and so this is what you were given. Something that seemed to be very complicated to many, something that had all kinds of ritual, information that had hierarchies, levels of angels, you know?

But now, there is a great need for simplification because you are not any longer working from an intellectual level. For most of you, it is from a heart level. And the heart needs simplification.

J: So we're really becoming more self-actualized. And because of that, we have a different response to angels.

I: Indeed. Humans have progressed to the point where they need the positive desperately.

J: Right. No longer will we associate angels with fear and wrath and that kind of experience.

I: Again, we comply. You need to learn to allow, to accept. Give yourself time and ask for experiences to come. So many humans put time limits on all that they wish to do, and you have closed the door to that side of yourself that is a vibrational frequency to see everything else. When you are born you have that, but you slowly begin to close the door. There are many of you on your planet who are what we consider blind and deaf, and it will take them a great deal longer to open back their doors. You cannot have a time limit for seeing. And to see is with the heart. It has nothing to do with intellect or eyes. And the heart is the one area where you need to allow.

J: It seems to me that we have been living out of our heads, and our hearts are not connected to our minds.

I: Again, that is part of the progress. You need to experience that so you can experience the other part of balance.

J: That is what we're striving for, balance?

I: Indeed. For many years you were in the intellectual area, and now you're beginning to go into the emotional area, the heart area. That's where you create the greatest growth.

J: And that's why we're experiencing more with angels because that's who they are. They're total love.

I: *And we will tell you a secret.* That is why you're experiencing more sorrow, more anger, more pain and more fear. When you begin to experience with the heart, then you begin to experience with the emotion, is that not so? And when you begin to experience with the emotions, do you not see that there has to be negativity in order to experience?

J: Well, I guess there has to be duality, for sure.

I: If everything were totally positive, would you even think about it?

J: No. We have the whole range of emotions, then, that we're dealing with, not just the ones on the positive side, but the negative ones such as violence and hatred.

I: Indeed, that is balance, is it not? And what do you feel, do you think first with your mind or your heart when you see a child has been murdered?

J: Oh, first with the heart.

I: That is what is so very important about this time period. Instead of just thinking, you must begin to feel. Whether it be anger, love, or any emotion you care to identify, if you do not begin to feel emotions, *really* feel them, you will not begin to allow. Now we must tell you that on this path, many of you strive not to have feelings at all about anything, and we must say to you that is denial and fear.

J: Yeah, I'm thinking of a friend of mine who stays un-ruffled all the time, and she thinks that she is in total peace and serenity and has life so in tow.

I: She is in total denial. You cannot be human and not feel. You cannot grow and not feel. You cannot progress and not feel. You see, emotions mean movement. When there is an absence of emotion, there is no movement.

J: And then there is no growth. So we have to reconnect, keep those emotions going and take them out now and then to analyze what they mean and what path they're taking us down, right?

I: Indeed. And, in fact, if you have an upsetting emotion, let us say your mate has not given you what you need, then you need to examine why you need that. You need to examine why you have the emotion in the first place, and you need to grow from that examination.

You need to get down to the bottom of the emotion. Most humans tend to go on one or two levels, but you need to keep asking questions until there are no answers. For example, you worry about finances, do you not? Why?

J: Because I have obligations, bills, and things I have to do with that money.

I: Indeed. But let's go down further than that. What would happen if you did not meet your obligations?

J: Well, there would be loss of things I can't keep up, like a house payment.

I: So you have a loss of material possessions? How does this make you feel?

J: Needy—on a survival plane.

I: Why do you feel needy?

J: Because I have to find a way to eat, and I don't want to depend on somebody else.

I: Indeed. And why do you wish independence?

J: Because I don't want to be a burden to society or to anybody else. I guess pride is the bottom line.

I: Indeed, it is not the bottom line. Why must you have pride? Why must you be someone who is independent?

J: That's a value I've chosen as important.

I: Why must you have this value?

J: I guess I chose it as a child.

I: And why must you have a value at all? Does this not describe who you are? Does this not mean how you get your affection, your love, and emotion? And so if you choose to be needy, and you do not have all those things that make you someone to be loved, what do you have?

J: Unhappiness.

I: And what is unhappiness for you?

J: Not being loved.

I: Indeed. Now you have gotten down to the very bottom. We would say that in 90% of all cases of humanness, the greatest fear is rejection and aloneness. And that is what most of you deal with on an every day basis.

J: But, why do humans persist in this "aloneness?" Why do we think that we're in this just by ourselves? Can't we sense that we're interconnected to everything?

I: Because they are afraid to be worthy of others' love. Be it animal love, angelic love, human love, God's love. They have this great fear that they will not measure up to that emotion. Love is the most powerful emotion of mankind, and they are always afraid that they will not be worthy of it.

Human or Angel?

Given the human condition which seems at times so painful an existence, it's a wonder why angels would choose to become human. Isabelle explained.

I: There are many souls whom you choose to call "impatient." Some humans love to live lives very calmly, serenely, and some learn to live life on your coasters.

J: Roller coasters?

I: Indeed. Well, that is about what it's like on this side. Some souls choose to experience those things that do not cause a great deal of consternation. Some souls choose to go for the gusto. There's a tendency for these souls to want to have it done, have it all over with, very quickly. And they think that they can learn so much faster by having those qualities that you call good and bad, positive and negative.

J: So, they think that the earth plane is an accelerated place for learning.

I: Indeed. Furthermore, at any point an angel can go into a sphere or a frequency and experience all that you have experienced. It is a vibrational thing. They can converge with the vibrations and experience that, too, but most angels do not choose to put themselves through those vibrations. It is not comfortable to some. Some do not wish to feel emotion.

You see, when you are in a vibration where you do not have to experience the polarities of good and bad, right and wrong, positive and negative, then you also do not have to experience the emotions. The only emotion that I can tell you that angels experience is unconditional love. And, as such, angels choose to love humanity in that way.

Life Before Life

For those of us who believe in "life before life," it is reassuring to hear that our guardians were assigned to us before we took on human form on earth.

J: At what point do those of you who are our guardian angels come into our lives? At the time that we are conceived or at the time that we need you?

I: *Can we tell you one other secret?* You have a secret life. It's before you are born. And that is when guardian angels come to you.

J: So they're there with you as you're being born.

I: Would you like to take a trip where you have forgotten your money or your car? Then why would you take a trip and forget one of the most important things to you: help. And so, these things are planned before you are even conceived.

Even a fetus in the womb is in communication with its guardian angel. Some souls undergo the entire process of being conceived and born, but then opt not to complete their mission. But even these have guardian angels.

Heaven Only Knows

If a worldwide survey could be taken of our individual descriptions of heaven, we'd have as many pictures as we have people. Isabelle claims that whatever image we believe in is what awaits us.

I: Each and every soul has in its philosophy, heart, and mind, what heaven is, and that is what it becomes.

J: It's all from our perspective of what reality is, right?

I: Indeed. In this little one (Rosie), there is a perception of a garden with beautiful flowers and no allergies which I find interesting. In your perception, it may be something different, maybe a place to learn, a place to grow at a pace that is fast and far superior to your own on this side. In another's perception, it is a resting place, or it may be a city with your St. Peter standing at these beautiful golden arches. In other's perceptions, it may be a giant mall.

J: (laughs) A shopping mall?

I: Indeed. Where you have a gold card.

J: And shop 'til you drop.

I: And you never have to drop.

J: (laughs) That's great.

I: In another's perception, it may be freedom from a body that has been so crippled that one cannot fly. And in another's perception, it may be youth and beauty. So it is whatever you choose to make of this. And, in some people's perception, it is fire, it is grayness, it is mourning, it is crying out.

You see whatever you choose to think of yourself when you pass over; whatever you choose to think of the place that you are going, you will begin to see that. Until you choose to change that pattern of thought, then it will be.

J: Rosie told me one time that she was talking to my father who's been on the other side now five years, and that he was building a house, so that was his perception of heaven.

I: Indeed. And what was interesting is that this soul knew that he could think this into being, but chose not to. He is a personality who needs to work, to feel with his hands, to see progress, but in reality if he chose to think this house into being, it would be there like this. (Rosie snapped her fingers.) But this human being needed to feel progress and that's why he's building.

Isabelle explained that what we call heaven, they call the fourth level, and it's a dimension that allows us to create anything, mold new bodies or create instant sunshine just by thinking it so.

I: You do not even have to wish. It is a thought process. You might think of a fine sunny day, and you will have a fine sunny day.

J: Gee, that's great!

I: *We tell you that is a secret* because so many of you would be coming over.

J: (laughs) Would it be too crowded over there?

I: No, it is a vast empire. But when you get tired of playing with the body, you begin to play with other substances, your energies, your power, what you can make out of nothingness, and then that becomes old hat, too. So you choose to go on. It is the beginning. And as you choose to go on into other levels of thought processes, you do not need the body. And then you can become what you truly are and that is energy.

J: So it's kind of like heaven or the first step on the other side is Grade 1, and then you just keep going up from there.

I: *We'll tell you another secret.* Our side's a school house, too. There never is a place where you do not learn.

J: It's continual learning.

I: Indeed. It is, your term, eternity. Or infinite.

J: Infinity?

I: Indeed.

Cremation vs. Burial

People who espouse burial over cremation usually have a religious reason by their preference, but Isabelle states that it's not the way we're buried; it's our belief system that affects us on the other side.

I: There are many who have come over here, who have lost parts of their bodies, and who have insisted for a long time to come that they still do not have that part with them. It is a gentle laughter that we have for these souls because they do not need bodies at all.

But again, it is the philosophy that was given many thousand years ago in ways that human beings could understand. Before this time, there was a great deal of cannibalism which was not always a good thing for other human beings because diseases were carried in this way.

And so many philosophies sprung up in order to do honor to the human being and also to keep other human beings from carrying disease, from having them deal with the blood of those who were diseased, and so they were buried. There are many different cultures who believe in many different things, and it is all superstition—all of it.

J: So, it doesn't really matter.

I: It does not matter. If you wish to think of being buried one day, you might think of ending up on a shelf because your land has no expansion. There is not enough of it even now. And so at some point all those souls who had grand ideas of carrying their bodies with them at the ending and at new beginnings are going to find them up on shelves.

There is so much pollution in the human body at this time from your hormones, chemicals, the things you ingest, your stress even, that it would be a good idea to purify as much as possible. And it is not for your soul on this side because what you perceive on this side is what your thought process is. But it is rather for the human beings left behind.

Better to be sure to purify most of those things that you call human elements in order not to have so much in your ground.

J: Do away with pesticides, food additives, preservatives, those kind of things.

I: This shall not happen for approximately 100 years, but you will be advised to do away with the human body because it contributes to the pollution of the earth.

There'll be many of your souls on that earth plane who will choose to think of this as totally full of baloney, that's your word, baloney. That is an interesting conglomeration of stuff.

J: (laughs) It is, and it's not healthy for you, either.

I: Basically, to tell you the truth, your human body is baloney. So, in order to help other human beings who come after, it would be a good idea to purify as much as possible because it does contaminate the ground that you walk on and you grow things on. You'd be surprised what you would find in your bones even now.

You Can Take It With You

When we are preparing to take on human form, we not only have the guidance of angels, but libraries, hospitals, and other institutions at our disposal.

I: How could you explain someone who can come to your earth and play beautiful music at the age of three? How could you explain so many prodigies? We must tell you that those souls do not have it easy. They work very hard to get those lessons down, to get their talents honed to a fine degree. And they tend to do that even on our side.

We do have great universities. You see angels or souls who have a higher vibration, have a tendency to be very bored doing nothing. They tend to love to learn and experience. There is any source of education that you choose to desire. If you choose to invent in a lifetime, it will be done here first.

J: When you're born on this plane, do you bring that experience from the other side with you?

I: Sometimes. Sometimes you choose to have a personality or a soul, let us say that—it is hard for us because they are all vibrations, all energy, but there are many good friends on this side—and so there's a tendency for a soul to say, "I will whisper into your ear and help you from that side in this way."

Chapter 3

Crossing to
the Other Side

*All lifetimes will be opened up to you so that you can see
all that has been done since the beginning.*

The Death Experience

O nce we are done with this life, we discard the body
like taking off an old coat, and we step into "the
other side." Numerous accounts of people who have
had near-death experiences all confirm similar images of light
and wonderful feelings of love.

I: Think back to when your child was born. What was the feeling at the moment of birth? When you looked into your son's eyes the very first moment.

J: I felt total wonder and joy.

I: Indeed. This is somewhat how those who have had the experience of near-death experiences feel. It is as if everything is finally explained. Everything has been worth it. Everything is in its place. And there is great wonder and joy at the idea that things are not so terrible or bad.

J: When we cross over to the other side, what awaits us?

I: We await you. There are varying degrees of differences when you experience the death process. And those of you who feel that you have been a very bad or evil person begin to be very frightened and very confused at the moment of death. There is a vibration that you put out into the atmosphere and it is of fear, guilt, all those confusing feelings. And you may find yourself in a place where you feel those vibrations greatly.

But let us speak of a beautiful little old lady who has given her life to be of service, who has loved greatly and tried to do the thing that was best for all. When that person chooses to cross over, what she shall usually see is a beautiful, warm, glowing light. It is a light to bathe in. Then she begins to see shapes that you consider human. (If you were of another species, you would see that species.) And then there is a great welcoming, a celebration. There is much laughter and joy and tears that another has come home. It's as if you have been away for a long, long time and you are welcomed back into the family. There is a great sense of belonging. By the way, most of you choose to come over with the body. It is not really there, but in your mind's scope it is there and so it is allowed.

Fear of Dying

Even though the ecstatic experience of the light as we pass over to the other side is so compelling, we are still so afraid of dying.

I: Because most of you have gone through that veil you call forgetfulness. Why do you have fear of stepping into a darkened room at times?

J: Fear of the unknown, I guess.

I: Indeed. What if there is something there to reach out and grab you? And because the organized religions of your world have a tendency for the very first thought process to be negative. I might have done something 25 years ago that I should be ashamed of, you understand? And so, that is why most humans are afraid. Another thing is that most humans, no matter what type of life they are living, choose to have life.

However, it is comforting to know that our guardian angels as well as others reach out to help us make our transitions.

I: *We will tell you another one of our secrets.* Your guardian angel comes in before you're even committed to be human, to commit to your soul. Your guardian angel is there when you leave, and it commits to your soul to help you out. That is the angel who is in the forefront, but many others are around you. There are many helping hands on our side, you could not count them all, in order to help each and every one. There is even a soul, and we do not say necessarily angel, but a soul who commits to be that which you choose to see. Let us say, for instance, that you have a great deal of religious philosophy, and you choose to see your Mary or your Jesus or your St. Peter. This is what you will see and sometimes souls take on those roles for you.

J: So, it's not necessarily the angels themselves but emissaries.

I: It is a part of the energy of the soul you call St. Peter. It is as if the soul takes on the cloaking, the energy of the soul that you wish to see. It's like a blending.

J: Like the Vulcan mind meld (laughs)...Star Trek. It's a television show that we watch where one species blends its mind with the other.

I: In your picture boxes.

J: In our televisions.

I: That is a wonderful way to turn off your brain.

The Party's Over

When the reunion is over, and especially if their death has been particularly traumatic, people will recuperate in rooms of special colors and warmth to rest for whatever time they choose.

I: When a soul chooses to go on from the resting place, then that soul will always have a guide to lead the way, always. You go into a level that you consider judgment. That is approximately a third level where you are given the very fine opportunity to review your processes, the life and lessons that you have chosen, and what came to pass in your life.

Now there are a great many souls who choose not to want to do this. For most humans—again we will exclude other races because they do not always have the same thought processes humans do—we would say 80-90% choose to believe that there must be something negative about themselves. Your word "bad."

And so there is a tendency for them to wish not to look at their life. But with much coaxing, persuasion, and gentleness, they get to review. And again you are asked to make a judgment of how you did, like a report card from school. But you see, the teacher is not someone from the outside. The teacher is from inside—yourself. And so you must give yourself a report card, and this is one of the hardest things to do.

Let's say you were to go to a giant garage sale and see this lovely vase or object of art. And since there is no price on it, you ask the person who is selling this fine quality merchandise, "How much is this thing?" And that person said to you, "Make me an offer." Do you realize how hard that is to do?

How many humans do you know that would say immediately, "Oh, five dollars" or whatever. Most humans tend to say, "Oh, I don't know. I would rather you choose."

And this is the process much like what we do on our side. You must make an offer on your soul and at a cost that many souls become very frightened about. And so they say to God, "No, no, you must do this thing for me." And your God chooses not to do this, but gives you the fine opportunity to weight your soul yourself, and it has nothing to do with punishment. It has to do with the fact that souls tend to need lessons. They tend to need to perfect themselves. They tend to need balance. And all this is by these souls' choice. It has nothing to do with your God.

Judgment Day

J: Going back to the lessons learned as we review our lives, there's a book out by Dr. Raymond Moody which I think is called *Life After Life*.

I: He's a very fine man. He is trying to bring back clear consciousness of the idea of immortality.

J: Well, he says that at the end of our life, when we're doing this review, there's a test with only two questions: What wisdom did you gain and how did you expand your capacity to love?

I: Indeed, that is true. But what you must do is go beyond that. Why are these questions asked?

J: So that we will learn for the next life, I guess.

I: Indeed. It is a question that is asked in order to assimilate all that has been said, all that has been done, all that has been known, in this last life. And the purpose of wanting to know what it is that you have accomplished on all vibrations, the physical, mental, and emotional is so you can assimilate what is yet needed to be done. It is not a form of reward or punishment or a form of condemning. It is assimilating all that has been done to date.

Now when the life has been judged and it has become known as to what to work on in the future, then all lifetimes will be opened up to you so that you can see all that has been done since the beginning and then you can assess what is needed in your mind's future.

Those souls who abort their mission early by committing suicide still have to review their life's lesson and eventually complete it in a future lifetime.

J: Is it worse for them because they took their own life?

I: It is not worse. It is confusing. It is as if you were in a fog in San Francisco. Have you been in a fog where you could not even see the signs?

J: Yes.

I: Do you not feel confused and alone? That is what you would experience to a point. But there are always kind, loving souls who surround those people and want to touch, hold, and love them, but most of these souls choose not to look or feel. They choose to be in confusion so they do not have to deal with their own lights.

Then there are souls who come to us with addictions, be it food, sex, alcohol, drugs, anger. Those souls are also in what we consider a very gray area. But they continue to try to experience humanness, and it is something very sad to see because they will not reach out a hand in order for us to help them. But until they do, we cannot have judgment. We cannot force our will upon them. We can stand by and, as you say, wring the hands.

J: Does Elvis Presley fall in that category? Because it's been speculated that he accidentally killed himself with an overdose of drugs. Is that considered a suicide?

I: Your soul that you call Elvis Presley had been trying to do that for many years, but he had a tendency to love to live near the edge. He liked your roller coaster rides, and he loved to dare the universe to see if he could win. It was like playing Russian roulette. He knew very well what he was doing, but he was so self-destructive that he could not help himself. And there are no accidents.

Yes, he is in a very gray area, but there are many souls who are constantly sending up feelings of warmth, love, and joy for this soul, and he is resting at this point.

J: What exactly do you mean by a "gray area?"

I: It means that he feels the need to atone for his sins to his body. We do not say that this is something he needs to do. This is something he has taken on himself.

J: Right. As a choice.

I: Indeed. There are some of you who choose to come over and to feel as if you had made many mistakes and need to atone for those mistakes. And when those souls come over like that, there is a tendency for us to comply and allow for a time, but at no time do we not try to persuade that entity that all is well and that they can go on.

J: Well, people really love him and continually send him prayers.

I: Just by the fact of loving, you send up messages, you send up compassion, you send up just about any type of emotion you can think of and that all is to the good.

J: So, will that help Elvis get out of his gray area and to the light?

I: Indeed, it has, but this is a soul who is very weary and feels very misused. You could imagine that this soul has gone back to being a very small child and needing that type of attention. And there are many souls around this one to help that.

J: I imagine he's with his mother.

I: Indeed.

J: Well, that's good. We wish him well. What about the actor John Candy? He was really overweight and died at a fairly young age, 43. That wouldn't be considered suicide, would it?

I: Indeed, it was not. It can be considered an addiction, a feeling of self-worth, but the purpose of this soul had been completed. This soul came to show compassion, gentleness and happiness to others who were in the same condition. This soul on a personality level had an addiction. But on a higher level, this person chose that addiction in order to help others overcome their feelings of sadness, of self-worth.

J: Yes. People could look at him, love him, and feel good about themselves no matter what size they were because he was so filled with joy.

I: Indeed. And sometimes the very act of death, of giving one's life to a purpose will bring about more progress than one can on your side. Many souls will be thinking about changing. Many souls will be thinking with compassion which is something that might be new for them. Many souls will be sending up prayers which may be new for them. And many souls will be speaking with joy about that life. And that is the purpose for this one.

J: He had completed his mission.

I: Indeed, he had.

What About Hitler?

The idea of having to account for everything we have ever said, done, or felt is a fairly terrifying one for the average person, but what about someone like Adolph Hitler?

I: You must understand something important. This is a soul who chose to take on a great lesson for your world. This is a soul who caused a great deal of death and destruction. But it was also a great lesson. And while this soul had to look upon that life, this soul also did humanity a justice.

J: In what way?

I: In that there are no negative and positive aspects on our side, this soul helped to teach humanity a great lesson. Through all of that turmoil and pain came great lessons of compassion, did they not? Through all that destruction came many lessons which your physicians learned to help others. Through all that pain came the lesson that we cannot ever allow this to happen again and that humanity must help each other.

While some of you do choose to forget at times, the great majority of you do not. If you did not have that war and destruction, how many people do you think would think about those souls who are worse off than themselves, those who are different, those who have handicaps? That lesson was great, indeed.

And while this soul had a lot to look at in judgment of self, this soul also did a great service to humanity and brought humanity forward approximately 150 years.

You see, that is what is different about our world and yours. We do not consider lives lost because they have not, in reality, been lost. And every one of your wars has had more than one purpose.

J: What happened to Hitler after he reviewed his life?

I: He came to be a contribution to humanity in one form, but after you get onto the earth plane, even though you have a plan, you can take that plan to extremes. You can choose not to do it or you can do it to the extreme. The role of being a provider for a grand lesson is one thing. But it is how you do it, how you recognize that role, how you act with that role, that makes, in your words, karmic debt.

And since this soul went past the prescribed commitment, he needed to look at those things that came about. This is a soul who recognized at one point that he had gone too far with the commitment and has had great feelings of loss for himself.

J: But if there is no punishment on the other side, what would motivate us to refrain from being bad?

I: We did not say that there was no punishment on the other side. We said that your Hitler chose to commit to a lesson that had a great deal of advancement for your race. We also said to you that there are some who choose to commit to a lesson, and go past that lesson.

But we did not say that there is no punishment on this side. We do not tend to think of these things in terms of punishment. It is humans who tend to think in terms of punishment.

But you will be encouraged to look at the entire life and once you do so, you will also look and feel at what happens to the other side of things. When you have done something to another personality, and that personality has been damaged from it, you will have every opportunity to look at the damage and to feel how it felt to be damaged in such a way.

J: So you can choose to feel what they felt?

I: You do not choose to feel. You choose to look at it. That is why there are so many souls in a gray area, because they have the fear of looking.

Let us ask you, when you were a small child, and you bit another person, and your mother explained to you that this hurt the other child, and you saw the tears of that child, and you began to be aware that this was not a good thing to do, and you began to feel awful that you might have hurt someone, they were in tears, and you really liked that person. You are made aware of what your actions have caused.

And that is very much what it is like on this side. Some of you may think of this as a form of punishment and some may choose to think in terms of advancement. It depends on the mind. There are many souls that we have complied with who choose to say that they need to be in your word "hell" at this time. And we comply with that. If there is a wish to be punished, then we comply.

J: Because that frees them up from all this?

I: Because that is their judgment of themselves. Until they are ready to accept different forms of advancement, then they must do as they see fit.

But we did not say that you would not have some sort of reckoning. It can be very interesting to see what happens to another person who has been damaged with thoughtless words or by actions that are thoughtless. And you are made in this way to feel what it feels like to be damaged by another in that action. When you look at something and you cannot turn away from that, then it is a way of making you feel what it feels like to be damaged.

And also we must tell you that it's not all negative on this side, negative actions, negative thoughts. There are a great deal of positive thoughts and actions in each and every human being and that, too, is shown.

J: So, they look at their whole experience in totality.

I: Indeed, and on top of that, you will be able to see how a personality felt when you did something unexpectedly kind for another. You will see how the person felt when another human being cared even a bit for him. The swelling of the heart, the feelings of thankfulness, the embarrassment even that someone could be as kind to him as you were. You will be given that choice to do that, also.

J: That's neat.

I: Indeed, it is. But the greatest forms of punishment do not come from God or your devil. They come from yourself, and if you choose to think of them as punishment, it will be complied with. If you choose to think of them as advancement and what to work on in the next time period, that will be complied with, also. Whatever's needed here and whatever is recognized, is not wasted.

Now we say to you that your personality of Hitler did, indeed, have to look at his lifetime. But he had gone past the recommended cut-off. And he got carried away with his own power. And so he misjudged the commitment. And, indeed, he was able to view everything that happened and so in our world, he had to look at all.

For instance, there have been many medical experiments in that time period done on human beings that were indeed very cruel. But through those medical experiences come great advancements in your history of medicine. And each and every human being who perished in those war years committed to do so for their own advancement. And so coming from evil, as you humans call it, comes good, balance.

Karmic Debt

J: Can you go into karmic debt for a bit, and touch an how we accumulate it? Does it only happen when the soul oversteps its bounds for the lesson it was supposed to have learned?

I: A lot of people think that karmic debt means that it is a pay-back, a reward or punishment system. This is not so. Karmic debt, karmic bonds, are a way of processing your polarities. If you have, let us say, a lifetime where you choose to commit the worst murder, at that point you incur a debt of experiencing the other polarity.

J: Which is to *be* murdered?

I: Indeed. For example, personalities have lived with personalities throughout many lifetimes and they incur karmic debt, in your terms, they choose to experience jealousy, then they may work on other lifetimes where they each have to experience the opposite.

But, at one point, there will be a need to let go. And by the very thought of saying to yourself, "I need to let go of this act of jealousy," the karmic debt is completed.

That is the interesting thing about humans. The intention of allowing this negativity to leave is a cutting off period, but most human beings do not feel that it is so. They do not realize that it is completed, so they will spend many years trying to take off this debt when it has already been completed. It is like paying for a fine house and not having the realization that the debt is paid off, and you continue to make your payments for years after.

The intent to do something is as much as doing that deed. In fact, the intent is far more important. We have many human beings who choose to come to the light and review their lives and are very surprised when they see their thought processes carry as much weight as their actual deeds.

And this applies to a personality who chooses to do something good for another soul. Let's say you plan to give a Christmas food basket to a needy family. You go about your day, buying food and canned goods which you have planned all month to do. We say to you that this is not as important as when you reach in your pocket and give one dollar to someone for a burger. Without planning, without thinking. Out of the kindness of your heart.

Now the food basket is also a kindness of the heart, but it is a plan. It is something someone carries out for a reason. But, when someone reaches into the pocket and gives a dollar, saying, "Go get some food. You look like you need it," it is unthought of. It is a kindness of the whole.

J: Like random acts of kindness.

I: Indeed. Those are thought of much more importantly than deeds that are planned because when you plan a deed, there is a tendency for there to be a condition.

J: You want something back.

I: Indeed, you do. Let's say you plan a food basket. What do you think you get from that food basket as a pay-back?

J: Gratitude.

I: Not only that, but you get the feeling of satisfaction for yourself, do you not? But when you do a kind deed without thought process, what you receive back without thinking about receiving back is joy. You feel your heart soar, do you not?

J: Well, you know, this happened to me last week. I saw an old bag lady on the corner when I was stopped at a light. She just looked like she needed some help. So I pulled my car into a gas station, got out, and put my hand on her shoulder and said, "Can I help you in some way?" She started rattling about wanting to meet with her family, and would I take her to a place about 15 minutes away. Was it on my way? And I said yes and put her cart in the back of my trunk and took her to where she wanted to go.

She wouldn't accept any money I offered. I gave her a phone number for help so she could stay at a shelter and get food and a shower, but she didn't want to do anything I suggested. Finally, I told her I cared about her and let her go on her way. Now I didn't get any kind of satisfaction in the way that I wanted to because she wouldn't let me help her.

I: How did you feel when she took your kindness? Did you feel as she left your car a soaring of the heart, an uplifting? That is important for you to recognize. It is a different thing than satisfaction. That is saying to you the basic good of being human. That is as close as you can come to unconditional love on your earth plane. And you can feel it by a soaring of the heart.

And we say to you that the next time you plan to do a beautiful act of kindness, feel the same feeling that you feel when you do this. Calculate what it is you feel. Understand the difference. Feel the different emotions that you experience with both sets of kindness, and you will begin to understand what we are speaking of.

And that is why a random act of kindness is so very important, and we say to you at the beginning when those of you who care to listen to this voice and understand what we are saying, you will begin by planning random acts of kindness, but at some point, you will forget yourself and you will do this naturally. And then you will feel the soaring of the heart. That is the truth of humanness. The soaring heart is where you are really at. That is why you are here, to experience just that feeling.

Reincarnation

Although many of us profess a belief in reincarnation, we don't always agree on its definition. Miriam offered a clarification of our concept of reincarnation.

M: You have a philosophy on your earth called reincarnation. We feel that many people become very confused at this word. They have an idea that they live more than once. Now we must tell you something very serious. Let us say the personality of Jennifer, the personality of Bud, the personality of Robin, the personality of Rosie, shall never live again. But it is the souls that go on. It is not the personalities that go on. And that is why you can contact most anyone that you choose to contact on this plane.

The personality that is Jennifer shall never be again. It is unique. It is different. It is a wonderful personality, but it shall never be here again. When you choose to come to our side, you will take off the shadow called Jennifer and put it away, and then the soul shall be clean and whole and take on another.

We do hope that we have cleared up a little bit of that. It is important for people to know that they shall not come back in any form that is them, except maybe a bit of rememory. And also some of the fears, for that stays within the soul as a way of something to work on.

J: So, could it be that some of the traumas that you experience stay with the soul? For example, I'm thinking if you died in one life from drowning, could that memory stay in the soul so that maybe the next lifetime, you're afraid of water?

M: Indeed so. You see the fear is not the personality. The fear is a catalyst for learning. It is a tool, if you will. And so that can stay within the soul and what it means is that if you have that fear you must work on it in some time period, be it the personality of Jennifer or Richard or David, but the personality Jennifer has but one chance to deal with that.

Again, fear, happiness, trauma, anger, boredom, sorrow, none of that is a part of a personality. You do not come with it. You gain it. Through living. And so we need to tell you that they are tools, if you will, to balance the soul, to work them out, but they have nothing to do with the personality.

J: They're catalysts. So when we leave at death and cross to the other side, what is it that the soul hangs onto? What is it that is changed from each lifetime?

M: With the soul? It has some balance. That is about it.

J: So that's what it's seeking.

M: Balance, yes. Many of you think that the soul is seeking perfection. That is not true, my friends. You see, your Creator does not make anything that is imperfect.

J: So the soul is already perfect.

M: Indeed, but very few of you believe this, do you not?

J: Well, we've been taught in religion classes that that is not the case.

M: And so they do need work, do they not? They need to have a job. And again, as with priests and lawyers and doctors and any other type of human being endeavor, you all need those things to learn and so it is provided.

Going Back to the Whole

Once we have experienced lifetime after lifetime, all there is, we are returned back to the Source.

I: The object of your coming to and from lifetimes has nothing to do with perfection. How do you think you can be most like your God? It is not the idea to be perfect. It is the idea to experience all. So having experienced all, then you can experience the whole. And that is what it means by going back to God. If you wish to be as much like God as possible, that is what it means, the need to experience the all.

J: And what happens when you go back to the Source?

I: Have you ever seen a sponge? Let's say you have some water on the sponge, and you also have some on the cupboard. If you put that sponge very close to the water, what happens?

J: It gets absorbed.

I: Indeed. And it draws itself to the bigger entity, does it not? That is basically what happens in a simplified version. And then you experience ecstasy. For when you experience the all, then it is all known. There is no more to learn. It is all there.

J: And then what happens to you?

I: Then you become a part of the whole and the whole becomes larger. It has expanded.

J: So, everything is just expanding. The universe, all of us, God. Everything is just in a continual state of expansion.

I: Indeed.

J: And when the soul is back in the whole and blending, at what point does it decide to emerge again and go into another personality?

I: It does not leave after that. It becomes a part of the whole. It is not the most important thing to reincarnate on planets. There is work to be done even when you merge with the force that you call God.

J: What kind of work?

I: There is a great deal of creating. There is a great deal of helping others on this planet, on other planets. There is a great deal of work to do all through the whole, the universe, whatever you choose to call it.

You also need to understand that when the soul becomes part of the whole, it also does the work that you call God.

J: Which is creating and expanding.

I: Indeed.

Returning to Earth

For the most part, our choices for the next life, like when to be born and which lessons to be learned, are selected after the review process has been completed. But some souls run back to earth before finishing the process with the result that their lives tend to be very confused a great deal of the time. That's because a great change occurred after World War II.

I: There was a tendency for everything to need to go on to a higher vibrational level, for humanity to speed up, and for the experiences to speed up. And so there was a tendency for souls to feel the need to change their vibrational levels at the same time. And some of those who felt as if they had been cut off in their life's work tended to feel the need to continue. And so they chose to run back to the earth plane in the first vehicle that came about and incorporated a great deal of lessons and confusion in their lifetimes.

And it is happening much more frequently. There is a great need on our side to fulfill the expectancy of humanness. There is a great deal of hurrying at this time basically because humans have chosen to take what we consider the negative route. And so there are many souls who are trying to combat this.

Soul Mates

Speaking of impatient souls, Jennifer and her husband Bud are soul mates, defined as a spark of light so anxious to experience all there is, that it splits in two and hurries off to lifetime after lifetime.

I: Not everyone has a soul mate. Not everyone is an impatient soul. The reason for soul mates is that you have a soul who chooses to experience at a much faster rate. You call it impatience. And so this soul splits down the middle and experiences many life times, in half the time. And at one point, this little soul or part of the soul begins to be homesick for the whole. And so it incorporates lessons in lifetimes in order to become whole at a certain point.

The unfortunate thing about this is that soul mates may not always be experiencing the same lifetime. They may be experiencing different aspects even if they are in the same lifetime. They may be experiencing total opposites of what each other is experiencing and learning and when they come together, it is always not a very happy ending. It is not just the soul who comes into a relationship, it is a personality, also. And sometimes those personalities do not react well with each other.

But not all souls have soul mates, no, indeed. Some souls are not quite so impatient. And the purpose, the very purpose of soul mates, is because you have an impatient soul who wishes to experience on a grander scale, on a faster scale than other souls.

J: So, we split off at one point and just went out to experience everything we could possibly experience in an accelerated way.

I: But, as souls experience and as they live more and more times, there is a tendency to be heart sick because they do not feel whole, so they go about looking for themselves. For a part of themselves so that they can become whole. And unfortunately the soul becomes whole for that time period, but the personalities may be totally opposite.

Now we do see souls who have split and who have found their soul mates, who have identical thought processes and who converge and blend and become one, but this is very very rare, my friend.

J: Oh, I know. That's why I feel it's so rare to meet Bud because I feel we *are* soul mates and that we think so much alike.

I: Indeed, you are. But you are again experiencing different polarities, different lessons, are you not?

J: Yes. We still have to go through our lessons, but as far as the thought processes go, I think there's such an identity there. We just think alike in so many ways.

I: But you might think alike and see everything the same until the end solution. That is your personality, my friend. It is personalities who choose to come to different conclusions. And you do so because you have basic fears of control, love, rejection, any one of those things.

J: Yeah. Have we been together in different life times?

I: Many times.

J: In every kind of relationship?

I: Being seven.

J: Seven relationships. When was the last time?

I: We will tell you of one that was more interesting than the last time. Do you understand there is a power struggle between the two of you?

J: Yes. (laughs)

I: Do you know why? It is not because you are so individualistic with each other. It is not because you have your own issues. It is because at the time of France in the 16th century, this soul was your father figure and you were male. And he chose for you everything about your life.

And you ended up rebelling from this control and running away to what you consider service, army, feudal, with the guns and knives and all those things. This is a soul who remembers the controlling of the young son and chooses to want to lead the way again, to teach the other soul, to dictate and to lead the way. And, fortunately for this relationship, you are no longer the child. We do not say this is bad or good. We say that you need to find your own way.

Again, we have had a lifetime in England, 1802. Again, as siblings, sisters. A great deal of competition, a great deal of jealousy. A great deal of love, also. And the competition being that they chose to fight over the same man. This resulted in a death. That of your sister.

J: He was my sister?

I: Indeed, he was.

J: Did I kill him?

I: No, she killed herself. Because you won the personality that you both vied for. There was a great deal of remorse and guilt and it interrupted your life for a long time. Again, the last lifetime was as Americans. Again in a war. Fought on the same side. Both males. One being a surgeon, the other a calvary.

J: What was our conflict then?

I: There was not a conflict. There was a life-saving and then a death. This person that you were, being the surgeon, saved the life by amputation of the leg of the other comrade in arms. Then both were killed during an ambush when troops and those wounded were being transported to the back of the line.

J: Was it Civil War?

I: Indeed, it was. Let us ask you how you feel about cannon. Or bombs, as you call them now.

J: Don't like them.

I: Indeed. You were both blown to bits. And that is why there is such a repugnance. But, you do understand that even though this soul in this time period feels the need to be non-committed, there is something that makes him committed. (At the time, Bud and Jennifer were not married.)

J: There is something now?

I: Indeed. Why do you think this soul is with you if he does not want to commit to relationships?

J: Beats me. (laughs)

I: It is because there is a karmic bond, a pay-back for a life.

J: Oh. And, it was that last life, the Civil War life.

I: Indeed. You have gone through time quarreling, my friend, with this other side of yourself. It makes for an interesting relationship. We do not see one time being serene. There have always been things that you wish to work on together or against each other with. That is how you learn.

J: True. And yet, I just love to be with him.

I: That is because he is part of you, and it is part of the self that you are beginning to feel whole. It does not mean that you have the same minds or the same philosophies. This makes it interesting, does it not?

J: It sure does.

I: We say to you that if you had a love of your life, your soul mate, and everything was togetherness or the thought process was the same, there would be a tendency for you to be very bored indeed with each other. That is what makes it so interesting, these lifetimes of yours.

J: (laughs) It certainly is not dull. That's for sure. Now, when the soul comes in to experience all the lessons, does it have other functions or other levels other than just to experience lessons?

I: The soul comes in to experience all. The soul comes in to experience humanness. It experiences feelings of illusiveness. It experiences joy on a higher level. It experiences itself on a higher level. There are many reasons why souls choose to come in and to experience, but there are many experiences that you are not even aware that you are having.

J: Is it like Alan Watts says, that God is playing hide and go seek with Itself?

I: We would say rather that aspects of the God are playing hide and go seek with themselves.

Appearing from the Other Side

Sometimes our loved ones, including close family members and pets, appear to us from the other side, but not in the same form as when they left.

J: When Rosie's old dog Rusty died not long ago, she saw a vision of him going into a garden and becoming younger like a puppy. But later when she sensed him in spirit form, he was in his old body. Why did that happen?

I: There are two reasons. One is our reality and one is her reality. Let us ask you a question. As a human, do you not feel that there is always progression? And so, if you change that progression and go backward, does that feel right to you?

J: Not necessarily.

I: Indeed, it does not. It is a good feeling to know that a dog becomes healthy and alive again. It is a good feeling to know that, but it is not logical. You must understand that in our reality, everything is vibrant, strong, and beautiful. In your reality, that is confusing. And for the comfort of the heart there is a great need with this one to feel familiar with that vibration. And she does not feel familiar with the pup anymore. And so, out of the great love that that animal has for this human, this human will have what is needed.

J: And that's having the experience of the old Rusty.

I: Indeed.

J: I see. Well, it's similar to when my father passed to the other side. He had always told me that once you die, you die. For him there was no other side. And I had told him, "No, Dad, that's not true and when you get there, I want you to come back and tell me that." So about three weeks after his funeral, I dreamed about meeting him and he looked a lot younger. He seemed rather chagrined, saying "You know, you were right."

I: Your father chose to show himself younger to you for a reason.

J: And what was that?

I: Because with age, comes pain and his passing was painful to you. There was a feeling of helplessness and frustration that you could do nothing for this soul. And so, this soul chose to appear to you in robust health, so that you could feel comforted that he was no longer suffering.

Chapter 4

Our Origins

In fact, there was a combination of three different worlds who came to help seed this planet.

Mother Earth (How Do You Spell Relief?)

T he earth is a living being which has a soul and evolves as its own entity, as we do. Like us, it experiences positive and negative polarities, but it's definition of what's negative or positive doesn't necessarily match ours.

J: Is an earthquake the equivalent of experiencing a negative polarity?

I: Indeed, for the earth, it is not. It is the equivalent of a positive. If you have eaten something that is very rich or spicy, do you not have movement in the stomach? And is it a good thing for you to keep that movement into the stomach or do you let it out at least one opening?

J: At least. (laughs)

I: And why do you do this?

J: To be more comfortable.

I: Indeed. Or to stop the action of those spices on the stomach. To stop the pain. If you were not to let those gases either way out from the stomach, don't you feel that you would have a great deal of discomfort?

That is just as the earth experiences. Pressure is built up inside the core of the earth, and so there must be a way to let those gases and that pressure out. If there is not, then there is a great deal of discomfort for the earth sphere, basically because it has to go somewhere. And so, the earth, as a living, breathing organism needs to have relief.

It is natural for the earth to experience earthquakes, volcanic activity, and movement. But humans tend to think of it as a negative because those responses, those movements, are interfering with the way of human life. Humans are singularly the species who feel that everything should revolve around them.

Isabelle observed that our earth goes through twelve-year cycles of change and that there are other planets in other universes much older than earth occupied by some fifty million species!

Sacred Geography

There are many people who believe in the concept of "sacred geography," special places on the earth that seem to have a more spiritual link to the cosmos. Although visitors to places like Stonehenge and Sedona, Arizona, claim to feel a stronger vortex of energy there, Isabelle states that its people who bring the energy to these areas, not the other way around.

I: *We will tell you a secret.* It is not the earth or anything upon the earth that you call elements or that you call rock or dirt that is a force. It is what human beings bring to that place.

There have been many sightings of recent—you say— of the Virgin Mary. And it might be in a tree. And what happens is that many miracles start to occur, but have you noticed it is only after so many human beings congregate, pray, and put their energy into that place? This is what happens to most of your earth places that you call forces.

Now we do say that there are certain areas of your earth that have energy that is more so than other places. It is a way of letting out gases or vapors. It is a way of allowing the energy of the earth to expand.

But it is what human beings do with that energy. You see, the energy that the earth lets out has no polarities. There are no positive or negative forces. But you have a few people who experience a wonderful happening within that energy as they are standing by an apple tree one day. And those people will speak to others who will come and they will feel energy which they will begin to make into a positive force. And then it becomes a vortex or an open doorway to the other side.

And so your earth does not put out spiritual energy. It puts out energy. Just as you do as an aura, so does your earth. It is what you make that place. If you wish to take this wonderful little house that you have and say to many souls that you have a vortex in order to communicate with the God right here in your front room, and all who wish to participate may come and ask for healings, within two months you would have healings.

J: Because of all the energy that the people bring to the place.

I: And so there might be any place that has energy from your earth. It is like an aura. But what you do with that energy is something quite different, my friend. Have you not noticed that there have been places where you have gone in the past that did not seem to give you energy at all or made you feel wonderful or happy? But as more and more people came to that place for a meeting, the more you began to feel happy and energized. That is the principle we are speaking of.

We feel it might be a let-down to all of you souls who choose to feel that there is again another place where they can congregate to become wonderful human beings.

J: (laughs) That's true. What about places like the Pyramids and Stonehenge. What were their purposes?

I: Most of them had very strong purposes in science. You call it science now. They called it seasons. They called it a way of survival. They did many experiments and sacrifices. They did things in order to promote a beginning of a new day.

Your pyramids at one point were great learning centers and then developed into chambers for those very rich souls who chose to try to find immortality. But basically they were used for the alignments of the sun and the winter and the spring and all those seasons that come. The moon, the stars. They were gigantic learning centers.

J: There's a question as to how the Pyramids were formed. You know, some people claim that there were extraterrestrials involved in that and other people say that there were slaves brought in to construct them.

I: We will tell you that a bit of all that is true. There were extraterrestrials in the beginning, but they were not the Pyramids that you see today. They were the beginnings of pyramids. There were people from your city of Atlantis who came in and helped with some. Later on, when the human beings lost the idea of how to levitate, the idea of how to materialize those things that were needed, they began to use slaves.

J: At one point the Atlanteans *did* know how to levitate?

I: Indeed. It goes back before that.

J: How did they lose that ability?

I: Because they become afraid of not being able to control others. Say you have abilities, and you have a personality who wants to lead other people, and there always must be a leader. But if you have a leader who is jealous of others' abilities, there is a tendency to try to control those abilities.

And that is when some of your priests came into view. They would take those people, specialize them, single them out, and then they would be able to control their abilities. And as the people began to need these priests for different functions, they begin to lose their own abilities. And then they began to be told that it was wrong to use those abilities, that something very bad might happen to you. Again the human beings tended to listen to the negative. And so on and on it went.

Let us ask you this. In every single religion on your planet, but because you are from the Christian religion in the beginning, let us ask you this. How many of your religions say to you that is a wise and a good thing to get in contact with your angel and with your God? Or how many of them tell you that you need someone there who is wiser and who can be a teacher for you before you get in contact with your God or your angels.

You see what we are saying? Anyone, *anyone*, has the right to get in contact with their God and their angels, but how many are willing to do so? How many have fear that they might contact something else.

J: Or be ridiculed by other people. If you say, "I talked to my angel this morning," some people will just want to make fun of you.

I: Because they fear it, my friend. They do not laugh because they think it is funny. They laugh because they think it is uncomfortable for them and they fear what they do not know.

There has been conditioning throughout time immortal to believe that they cannot deal with these entities on their own because they might receive something bad. Again, the idea of the human thinking in the negative way. It is easier.

And look, this did not happen overnight. It happened over thousands upon thousands of years. Your Pyramids hold a great many secrets. There are great learning centers in the Pyramids. There are many hidden chambers, and you will find those eventually.

J: I always felt that in the King's chamber they did laser beam experiments on people, surgeries. Is that true?

I: Those were, as you were speaking, of the extraterrestrials, yes. But let us tell you that you have memory of that. And when you choose to feel stressed or tired, you may go back there and you may relive the memories, and it will give you energy. Again, it is a human being focusing their energies with the earth energies and with the memories, and you become one with all.

J: Yes. I found myself doing that at night when I felt I needed healing. I asked to be taken to the Great Pyramid and I could see myself in there laying on a stone where I was getting worked on.

I: Indeed. But it is a memory from the past and it is a way for you to tap into the past, and relive that memory as well as gain the energy from that memory. There is not a single amount of energy that has ever been, that is not still. As you were a human being in that lifetime, you are still a human being in that lifetime. There is still the energy from that humanness in that lifetime upon the land.

That is why places like your Sedona have great forces, force fields, around them. It is because many people created energy there. Many people prayed there. Many people chose to use their own energy for the good there. And it creates an energy field that does not leave. It does not dissipate. And when other souls come to that place, and they begin to have experiences, memories, then they too add their energy and so on and so on.

Our Evolution (The ET Connection)

There has been much speculation about the nature of our evolution as a human species, but the angels' version is that our past has no connection with being part-ape.

J: Can you shed some insight into our evolution? Were we as a human species ever evolved out of apes? It seems to me that we were our own species and they're their own.

I: Indeed, you were. Everything has become whatever it chooses to become from the very beginning of your seas. It has nothing to do with being part-ape. That is not so. There is a similarity of bone structures and brains, but it does not mean that your species at one time was ape.

At one point, this planet was seeded by other species. But that was millions of years ago and it started with your seas. It was not started from your earth plane.

J: Can you tell us who started it?

I: There are groups of souls who contributed to different species on your earth.

J: So some souls contributed to the plant kingdom and others to the animal kingdom?

I: Indeed. And others to the water kingdom. But where it began was in the water kingdom. And this was many more years than your scientists can believe at this time. But just as there are cousins in the animal world, those who belong to different species, let us say, the cat and the skunk, the cougar and all those different things, they are not one and the same, are they? They are cousins. That is why human beings relate to your apes and think of coming from those species. They did not come from them, but they are cousins to them. That is why there is a fury in your scientific community that there is a missing part.

J: But what's missing is our knowledge of how we evolved from the sea.

I: Indeed. Because there is somewhat of a likeness in your ape species, there is a tendency to believe that they are brothers. And this is not so.

J: So when we were placed as seedlings in the sea, how did we evolve from that point into land animals?

I: It took millions of years, but just as some of your species of fish evolved into different types of fish, so did these cells at the beginning. It was when the very first species crawled out of the sea and began to adapt itself to the earth. And in that time, there were mutations that mutated into other species. But all this was due to a planting of many, many different seedlings.

Safar, by far the most ebullient personality in the Isabelle group, enlightened us about the aliens who first seeded our planet.

S: These were not the only souls. Did you think there was but one? There are many universes or worlds who have come to help. In fact, there was a combination of three different worlds who came to help seed this planet.

J: Can you tell us more about that?

S: Your planet was very young at the time and there was a need to experiment as two of these populations were dying out. One population chose to need slave labor. And so they came together to try to create a world of those who were somewhat like themselves, but always on a lower level.

And they began to use different techniques of breeding. And so you know you have some wonderful mythology, did you know this? We say to you it is not myth.

J: About Zeus and Hera and...

S: Or your centaurs or your satyrs. Or those little people with the pointed ears. And no we are not speaking of Spock. In this one's mind, there is an image.

J: Oh, okay. So like the god Pan, half-goat and half-man?

S: Indeed. They were results of experiments that went slightly awry.

J: Slightly? So, it was basically to create slaves for them.

S: In one evolution. In one species.

J: And were we slaves then?

S: Some of you were.

J: How did that happen? I mean, did they come and get us, take us to their planet?

S: Indeed. They picked you up in their spaceships.

J: What about the Bermuda Triangle? We hear about this dimension where aliens can pick us up through that portal in the universe. Is that true?

S: There are many places that can happen. Yes, that is true.

Chapter 5

Multidimensionality

There will be a time period when humans will not
feel the fear of death. They will not feel the need
to protect themselves with anything but their
colors, their lights, their belief system.

Accessing Different Dimensions

Our true nature as human beings is one of multidimensionality, and we live in more dimensions than we can ever imagine.

I: There are some aspects of your body that live in the past and some that live in the future. The main aspect of your body lives in the present. But basically, because you must have these time limits or limitations, you choose to think of the past, the present and the future as separate realities, but we tell you that there are many parts of you that live in different dimensions, time zones or periods. Your scientists speak of such things as genetic memory.

And basically this is somewhat the same meaning of the aspects of living in the past in parts of your body. It is not truly a genetic memory. It is a part of you that is living in the past. But your scientists being of a left brain mentality tend to have to describe it as a final thing...a part of self that has no where to go. It is a finite thinking process, but it's much more complicated than that. And yes, there is such a thing as genetic memory, but there is much more of an aspect of living in different realms at the same time.

J: We have these different dimensions and what's considered real in each dimension has a different standard of measurement.

I: Indeed. What you choose to think of as not real is in reality very real. Let's say you have a small child and that small child thinks of monsters under the bed and in your reality, as a mother who is trying to deal with the child's fears, you would say there is nothing there, but the child knows there is something there because that is her reality. That is her thought process and so it becomes. And that is also in a different dimension. Just because another person cannot see the monsters does not mean they are not there.

J: So, we can say that supernatural creations like dragons, unicorns and werewolves really do exist in some dimension.

I: Yes, they do.

J: Why is it that some people have access to them and some seem not to?

I: Because some people wish to have access to them.

J: Does just wishing create that access?

I: Let us say wishing makes it so. Now, we will tell you that many of you can see the fairy folk, but many more of you say that there is no such thing. Indeed, there are fairy folk. It is just that some of you open your eyes wider. Every single thing that is thought comes into being. That includes your dragons and unicorns and things like that. Where do you think that people get the basis for these things?

J: Because on some dimension they *are* real.

I: Indeed, they are. And what you do to your so-called fantasy, your imagination, is you bring them into your reality. It does not mean that anything you think is fake or phony. It means that you are putting to effect those imaginations, those thought processes that bring other beings into your reality. Again, they are not solid, either. There is nothing in your world that is solid.

J: Except we tend to hold that picture of reality. We tend to think that everything is truly solid.

I: And do you know why? Because that is what the human mind can deal with. You choose to narrow your reality so that you do not have to frighten yourself or deal with those thought processes that cannot be comprehensible. And so there is a tendency for human beings to think just a little beyond their noses.

Dimension or Dementia?

As we experience new dimensions of reality, our standards for measuring what is real change drastically. For example, for those of us who live in the third dimension, our reality is measured by our belief system. If we believe it and it is based on our experience, then it is real.

In the fourth dimension, the standard of measuring reality is the intuition. If it feels right, then a person living in that dimension knows it is real.

Now how many of us are headed for the fifth dimension where there will be instantaneous knowledge? This is the dimension very much like where the angels come from, and where energy bodies will become needed. However, we won't all arrive at the same place at the same time.

I: There are different levels of your world that will encompass the needs of each and every soul. Some souls need—your definition—third dimension. Some souls need the fourth dimension. And some souls are reaching for the stars, the fifth dimension. And so at any level that you are, your earth will accommodate.

J: It's like when you mentioned before, the angels will comply to whatever our picture is. Is that the nature of the universe, to comply to whatever our picture of reality is?

I: Indeed, it is so.

J: And so, to change our reality, we change the picture?

I: To change your reality is to change your thinking is to change the picture of what your reality is.

J: And if we're the multidimensional beings that I think we are, then part of us is already out-picturing that, that planet 5,000 years from now.

I: *We have a secret for you.* Part of you are living that reality.

J: Really? That's exciting.

I: Do you find this strange? There are parts of you you cannot even be aware of. And there are aspects of self that live on our side.

J: Of *my* self? That live on your side?

I: Indeed.

Universal Dimensions

Some of us who are creating a new world out of our old one will not be on the same level of the world as it is now. It's as if we were looking in a mirror trying to see ourselves, and behind us is another mirror, so we see another picture of ourselves and another and another in the same mirror.

I: *We will tell you another secret.* There are many levels of your universe. It is not all things you know it to be. There are many levels.

J: So, all of it's changing at the same time?

I: Indeed, and some of it is changing at this level and there'll be some changing at this level (raises hand higher). You see, human beings are in progress. They're in movement. But there are some who are in movement at a different speed. And there are some who are in movement at a different speed from that, and so your universe is not the whole that you see. There are many levels of your universe, many dimensions of your universe, and it is not all as you see it.

And so as you take your world and you grow upon it, then you go into a different time span or level and then there is your world here and then there is your world here (raises hand higher). And so this world down here may not be functioning as this world is here. And you all occupy the same spaces. It is a level within a level within a level and it is something that is very hard to understand for most people. It is that you see.

J: Yes. It goes so far beyond the physical. There are many more levels, layers and dimensions than we can even imagine.

I: *And we will tell you another secret.* After you occupy the space of a higher level in your world, it becomes as solid to you as your world now is. And you leave this level of your world behind.

J: So, as we change our perception of the way things should be or could be, those levels change to match that perception. And as we leave behind the old picture, the new picture becomes solid and real to us.

I: Indeed, it does. And then when you get ready for another level, this world of yours is not quite so solid, my dear. It becomes more illusive and transparent.

J: More filled with light?

I: Indeed. And that is why some of you on your earth plane at this time are not in communication with the chaos. You do not touch the violence. You do not touch the chaos. You tend to see the light. And that is what we are saying. You are beginning to achieve a different level of a different plane of your earth.

J: Is that what Rosie means when she talks about light workers? People who work for the light?

I: Indeed. Although those are a specialized group of people who have come to bring the light, they have also come to bring a change to the level of the light. We try to explain it as simply as possible, and there are a great many of you who will not understand. But, when you see the light in yourself and when you see that your plane is becoming more and more transparent, and that things that happen in your plane do not necessarily touch your soul, then you will begin to understand.

There will be a time period when humans will not feel the fear of death. They will not feel the need to protect themselves with anything but their colors, their lights, their belief system. And even if one of them has been "smushed out," you will still not see that because you will occupy a different space.

J: And there won't be any need for qualities like trust because you won't have any distrust.

I: Indeed. Can you imagine that on your level at this time?

J: Well, I see evidence that that's not the case. There are so many wars, you know.

I: But, again, for those people who begin to see the transparency of the earth plane and begin to see that all can be let go, then you begin to develop another level of your world and you may not be on this lower level for a long period of time. That is why we have told some of you to touch not the emotions of others, but to live in thy own serenity. That is what it means. Live in your own level, your own light, your own glory and do not worry so much about chaos.

We do not mean to say that you cannot be an advocate of renewal, of letting go of this violence in your earth plane. We do not mean that you should not speak out. But you must not touch it with the soul. Because once you do, you become of the solid plane.

J: Yes, it just pulls you down.

I: It pulls you down to the level of the earth that is what you called at one point solid.

The 11th Level of Earth

What a surprise when David, an extremely enlightened soul from the 11th dimension, emerged from the Isabelle entourage, to tell us about the many dimensions of earth. Actually, there are 15 to 20 levels of our planet at this time, but we asked for a detailed description of David's level.

D: We come to you from that level that you call 11th in evolution, 11th in different dimensional thinking.

J: And how is the thinking different?

D: We do not have the chaos that your level has. We do not have the need for things that your level has. We do not have the need to heal another that your level has. We have learned to heal ourselves. We do not have pestilence or disease, as your level has.

J: But you still are on our earth and part of the earth?

D: We are within your dimension.

J: So, can you see, touch, smell, and taste, just like we do?

D: Most of the time, we do not wish to do these things.

J: Why not?

D: Because we do not need them.

J: How is your physical form different than ours?

D: We have become light-bodied. We do not need the sustenance that you need.

J: And what work do you do in the 11th level?

D: You would consider me "administrator." Our little ones you call children? We have those who set out in specific functions from the day they are born. And so, I do work to help those come along in different branches of what they wish to do.

J: So, you're kind of supervising the little ones.

D: Indeed.

J: If you have light-bodies, how do the little ones come about?

D: You are now, even now, experimenting with things that you do not understand with your processes of birthing. We have gone on further. We have taken the essence of two souls or two personalities and we incorporate it into... your term would be incubator.

J: Like we do test tube babies?

D: Indeed.

J: So that's how you generate the little ones. Are there lots of beings on the 11th level?
D: No, there are not.

J: Is it hard to reach the 11th level?

D: Is it hard to change your thinking?

J: You bet.

D: Can you conceive of the idea of changing your philosophies, changing your thinking at least 11 times totally?

J: Okay. So changing that many times, kind of evolving to the 11th level.

D: There is one interesting thing about us that you do not have at this time, most of you. We can come into spirit at any time.

J: You mean leave your bodies?

D: Indeed, it is an amusing thing, and we can converse with those on this side who have come from your levels and who have, in your terms, passed away.

J: Do all the other levels know about each other? In other words, do people from the 8th level know about the 11th and so on?

D: Let us ask you a question, my friend. Did you know about us?

J: Well, I knew that there were other dimensions, but I'm not sure how we can enter into them.

D: This is what is meant by going into a new dimensional thinking. It is going into another level of your planet. It is going into a planet that is identical to yours, but has a different thinking concept, does things differently, manages things differently. And that is what your planet is getting ready to do.

J: Can you explain a little bit further on how you think differently than us? Give an example of that.

D: There is not a great deal of physical work to do for us. A great deal of our work involves what you consider the mind. If we needed to build a very nice space to live, we would not do it physically. We would do it mentally. We can take the materials and elevate them into where they belong, you know, into the air.

J: Levitate?

D: Yes, we do many of these things. Most of us have our pet projects. We tend to enjoy things, to work at things that we enjoy. If you were to have a great love of teaching little ones, then that is what you would do. If you were to have a great love of reading, that's what you would do. Things are not supplied to us as they are to you. It is not needed. We do not need your vehicles. We do not need your fuel. We do not need a great many of the things that you need on your level.

J: How do you travel then?

D: We do it by mental telepathy.

J: So you just close your eyes and you can be anywhere on the planet or in any dimension?'

D: Indeed. But it is not comfortable to be in other dimensions because it is heavy. If you were to say to us, "Come and visit us," we would have to tie large boulders onto our feet. One of the great advantages of the level that we are speaking from is that we can converse with those that you consider on the other side.

J: Can you see them as well?

D: Indeed. This is where your planet, your level is headed.

J: We're all going to eventually be in that dimension?

D: And we will be at another.

J: What dimension are we in right now then?

D: The first level.

J: The very first? So we've got ten more to go.

D: You have much more than that to go. We come to you to tell you this basically because we were trying to explain to you what your guides were saying to you about there being many things that are unseen, that are not known, but they are there in reality.

There are many levels of your planet that have succeeded in what you wish to do. So there is a reason for hope. There is a reason for challenge. You see, what is happening, whether you know it or not, is that all of the levels are striving to come together, and so we come into the whole, also. It is not just one level that will come into the whole. It must be the entirety.

J: Our entire planet.

D: Indeed.

J: What happens then?

D: Then you can go on and become what you were meant to be.

J: Which is?

D: Gods.

David went on to explain about the specific lessons that are to be learned at each earthly dimension. For example, at level one our lesson is to let go of fear. In the second dimension we must learn to love one another, as Jesus said.

J: And what's being learned in the 10th level?

D: It is an opening. It is a way to evolve into a light being. Now, do you realize that when you talk about ascension, when you speak about coming into the whole, you might also be speaking about going on to different levels of your world.

J: I see. Is that what Jesus did? When he ascended?

D: Indeed. He has gone all through all the levels. And not just of your planet. As you go upwards to another level of dimensional thinking, then you can be reincarnated into that level for a while until you perfect that level. That is what perfection means. Until you deal with all of the experiences of that level, and then you begin to deal with experiences of the next level, then you can be born into the next level.

It is much more complicated than most people realize. It has nothing to do with just stepping from one place to another as easy as that.

J: Yeah. That's been the picture that we've always held.

D: That is because you are in the first grade. If we said to you, my dear, that is very good. You have perfected all the lessons that you came to learn from many lifetimes in this level and now you have risen to a second level of your earth plane, do you feel that that would be very wonderful in your thinking? Or would you wish to find that you are seeking a reward in your heaven?

For your people, where you are now in your philosophy, it would be a great let-down, would it not? If we were to say to you, oh my, you do not have the reward of blending into the whole, but you can graduate into second grade. It is not something that many souls would like to think about.

The one interesting thing about our level is that we have learned that there is no death in reality, and we can sidestep that fact. And when we choose to become tired, we choose to come over and to stay. There is no need to go through the dying process.

J: So between levels two through ten, we are just gradually becoming more and more aware of the need to let go of a lot of our assumptions, fears, and ideas of limitation, right?

D: Ascending into dimensional thinking, into many levels of your earth plane, is like taking off coats. You have many coats upon your back at this time, and each time you go into a higher thinking process, into a dimensional thinking process, you take off a coat until you have nothing to hide.

J: It's like taking off heaviness and becoming lighter at each step.

David commented on the angels and aliens on our planet who also go through the same process of experiencing all the dimensions.

D: There are some who choose to take a vacation and to learn faster. And they come to your planet to learn heavy lessons, indeed heavy lessons. And then they choose to go back to their own planets because they do not like the heaviness of your planet.

There are some that you call light workers that do not have to do any of this, but choose to so that they can experience humanness, and they tend to go from level to level to level. And then there are some who get so far and choose not to deal with it anymore.

At any time, on any planet, anywhere in the whole, anywhere that you are, you can choose to stay over on this side. But it is much slower in evolution.

J: How many planets are there?

D: Millions. When you consider that there may be approximately, let us say 100 of your earth planes in levels, you multiply that by others.

And each earth plane that you see is very much like the other except it is lighter. And on our level it is cleaner. There are not a lot of problems in the environment. The one thing that we come to tell you is that your earth plane will survive.

Chapter 6

Healing the
Human Spirit

*Laughter. That is the secret, my friend. If you begin to
laugh at yourself and at everything else, you will realize
how much easier it is to live—live through joy.*

Safar

The most colorful member of the Isabelle group was a
Persian ruler from 350 B.C. named Safar. A powerful
master who made life-and-death decisions dealing
with his subjects, Safar enjoyed great wealth, took solace in
food and sex, and had every pleasure at his fingertips. But
this life of luxury did not bring him any joy. People around
him schemed against him, there was much bigotry and

jealousy, and he couldn't trust anyone. Safar learned to trust himself, and heal his wounded spirit, a lesson he wanted to share with us.

S: I trusted in self and I trusted in animals. Pets. I trusted in the smallest flower to give me joy. I trusted in the sound of the water talking to me. There were simple pleasures for me. I was surrounded by opulence, and yet the simplest things gave me great pleasure and joy. And I learned how to take those moments of joy and put them into my heart.

And all around me, there was finery. There was gold. There was lapis. There was amethyst. There was anything you wished to have. There were those who wished to help me do anything that I needed to do. I couldn't take off my shoes. I was a person who was not allowed to be on my own. And so those moments that I took off by myself in my gardens, where my fountains were, where my animals were, I took great pleasure.

You see, the tiniest things mean so much. And it is a surprising thing to most of you in this time to think that one who could be so wealthy, who could have everything at the touch of a finger, who could have opulence surrounding him all through the day, all through the night, who could have the life and death struggle of others, someone living or dying, you would think in this time period, many of you, that that would be something that you wish to be, that that would be the greatest joy.

And we say to you it is not. For most of the time, when you have this opulence, you also have distrust. And you have others who are seeking the very opulence that you were born with.

And so, my friends, I learned to snatch at the smallest joys: the sound of a baby, the whisper of the wind in the trees, the smell of jasmine at night, the waterfall tinkling down over the rocks, the coolness of the grass, the coolness after a day of heat, a child's smile. All these things are there for the taking, and in me they created the greatest joy.

So, please do not wish for riches beyond compare that you feel so mighty. Do not wish for complete control over another human being because it leads to ruin; it leads to dissatisfaction and many times it leads to hate.

But understand that in each and every moment of your time on earth, you have a fine opportunity to create joy within self, be it a sunset or a sunrise, be it a petal of a rose with dew, be it your child's cry in the morning, and you know it has made it through another night safely.

Stop and compare that which you have that others might not. And at this time, we see much anger, much pain, for many of you have said unto yourself and others, "We have nothing." That is not so. You have eyes with which to see a sunset. You have feet with which to walk on the sand, to feel it between your toes. You have a mind that can contemplate the word "love." You have the ability to touch and to feel. To touch a furry lamb, to give an apple from your tree.

If you begin to learn through joy, you will see the countless blessings that each and every one of you has, down to the lowest soul. The ones who live in the sewer still have something that they can have to react with joy.

And when you bring this into your life, then you will bring much more. It is only when you begin to appreciate that which is given to you in the first place, that you begin to appreciate more.

There are those of you who cannot appreciate a thing in your life and it is unusual, but it is so. There are many wretches upon the earth in this day, but then that has always been so. But when you can begin to say, "I see the sunset. It is beautiful. I see a falling star and it is beautiful. It gives me joy right here in my heart," then it will bring to you much more joy, and you will bring to others joy also.

Would you like to know the secret of being? Of growth? Of being a human? You need to live in more joy. You need to be happier. You need to laugh more. You need to experience more jolliness.

It is an interesting thing about human beings on your planet at this time. From what we can see, and especially in the female element, there is a tendency to believe that what others think of you is so far much more important than what you think of yourself.

And we need to say to you: you need to lighten up. Every one of you. You need to enjoy who you are. You need to enjoy the light that you are. You need to begin to say: I am good. And it is so.

How many of you choose to say, "If only I had done the right thing. If only I had done everything that everyone wanted me to do." You must stop this at once.

If you wish to have a joyful life, to learn in joy, my friends, you need to be aware that you have to have joy to learn through joy.

How do you feel when you are having a happy day? How do you think other people see you? Do they want to be around you? Do they laugh more with you? Do they come closer into your space? Is this not so?

J: Yes, it's true.

S: And if you choose to do this as an experiment, you will find out how very much people wish to be around those who have great joy in their hearts and who enjoy themselves.

And if you could do this, you could live a much better life. It is as simple as that. Most of you tend to make living very difficult. You put so much in the way of your own enjoyment. And the greatest thing that you put in your way is what others think of you.

And if you could learn to think that what is important is what you think of yourself, you can live a much easier life, and you can have greater joy in your life. You see, even when you say, "I should not be this way," it is not through your efforts, it is through someone else's efforts to make you feel that way.

Teach your children to be joyous. Teach your children to laugh at little things including themselves. Teach your children to enjoy at a space of a moment that which they can't even see.

Laughter. That is the secret, my friend. If you begin to laugh at yourself and at everything else, you will realize how much easier it is to live—live through joy. And many of you would say, "But life is not joyous." Well, then, make it so.

You do not have to live in turmoil. You do not have to live in fear. You do not have to live in anger. You have a choice. And if you choose to take happiness over anger, fear, pain, and isolation, then you'll begin to know the true idea of living. And that is our message.

J: So joy is a choice?

S: Indeed, it is. Do you not choose to be hurt by another?

J: Yes. It's also patterns we get into, old habits.

S: But, you understand that our pattern is like a quilt and you can unravel it. String by string.

But there must be a beginning somewhere and so if you can stop allowing other people to make choices for yourself, if you can allow yourself to say, "I see my light. I see my joy," then you might be very impressed with your light and your joy.

You make the choice to be unhappy. You make the choice to be frightened. You make the choice to be joyful, and so we say to you find little things in life that can make you laugh, can make you shout with joy, and this, my friend, will become a pattern. And it will become one that is much tighter and much more fully loved than that one of fear and rejection. And so we suggest to all of you to begin to find a piece each day that you can laugh at, that you can enjoy, that you can say out loud, "This is joy." So that you can begin to understand it.

J: Yes. Sometimes just putting a smile on your face changes how you perceive everyone and how they perceive you.

S: And sometimes you feel angry, do you not? And sometimes you feel sad, hurt, or ill, but if you begin to search each and every day for a piece of what we find illusive in your world—joy—you will be aware that things can be much lighter, indeed.

And if you begin to do it when you feel all right with yourself and your world, then you will be aware that you can develop your own pattern, so those days that you feel unhappy, you can still look for that seed.

And this is the key, my friend. It is the key to disease. It is the key to anger. It is the key to stress. It is a cure- all, if you can think of it that way. Joy does not allow other things of a negativity in. And we say to you, try it.

If you have a time, a moment, when you're laughing and full of gaiety and delight, you will be surprised that there is not one negative thought that shall come in until you choose to let it. This was the thing that your forebearers knew quite well. They had joy in singing.

They had joy in talking with each other. They had community.

But because of your space, because of your energies that you have developed over the past hundred or so years, it has made you all isolated.

And so there is a tendency for you to have to find joy within each and every one, not within each other. And if you do begin to develop that wonderful emotion, joy, then you will have others who will wish to join you. And this will help. It will increase the world's sanity.

J: Yes. Scott Peck mentions in his book, *Further Along the Road Less Traveled*, that usually we come together in community out of trauma or some other tragic event and wouldn't it be wonderful if we could come together in community for a joyful reason.

S: Indeed. And if you can find one seed to laugh at, if you can find one small event to smile at and have gaiety with, you would be surprised at how many others will follow.

And you again need community. You again need to come together and express joy, laughter, a good time by all, love, emotion, touching. And yes, indeed, your world has come upon a great many remedies. Your age that you're in now is miraculous. But it has also done some severe damage to humanity and that, indeed, is a shame. For no matter how many antibodies you develop, no matter how many cures you develop, when you do not commune with another, when you do not have joy within your life, when you always worry about what others think of you, you will have disease. And it is not the ones that you cure. It will be others.

And so we say to you leave behind fear. Leave behind anger. Enjoy the secret of the ages. It is a mere thing, this thing called joy. But it can be the most wonderful thing in your world and you can make it. It is free for the taking. You can develop it in one another. You could do so much with that small word, joy.

And we say to you find the seeds, each and every one of you, and you will have the secret of the ages.

Gabriel the Archangel

One of the most profound experiences in interviewing Isabelle happened when the discussion turned to archangels and the Archangel Gabriel came in to deliver an important message of healing for humanity.

J: Gabriel, welcome. I am honored to have you here, and I would like to ask you a question. I know that you have appeared throughout our history. You were the one to deliver the message to Mary that Jesus was coming. Can you tell us more about the role that you play in our world?

G: Your Isabelle is correct in that we do specialize differently. I have come to deal with humanity's heart. Without heart, without the vibration of love in the heart, you cannot excel, you cannot go ahead in your progression. And so I chose to take on many souls in this part of your world as a way of trying to help your whole world.

J: How can we expand that feeling of love in our hearts? Are there some things that we can do on a daily basis that would help us?

G: First of all, humans need to cleanse this area. There is so much muck in this area at this time for most of you. You need to clean this area out before you can put the light in within the soul. The soul is behind what you consider the heart and it needs to have all of this area cleaned out. And then you can put that which you call unconditional love or light into this area. But you cannot do so when the whole area is festering with wounds and pus.

J: How do we clean that area?

G: We ask that you find a pink stone, in that pink is for your world a healing stone. And we ask for you to do this simple exercise. But we do warn you at this time that there are many who have felt somewhat traumatized by it. If you feel the urge to stop with this exercise, then do so, my friends. But, at some point, we do hope that you pick up where you left off. It is something that will be very good for you. Now for those of you who have extreme trauma, this exercise will take more than once to accomplish results and when you can begin to feel good about what you are saying in this exercise each time, then you will be aware that it is helping.

Take a stone that is pink. You do very well with your quartz crystal. Make it a large, smooth piece. Hold your hands as if in prayer, and put this stone in between your hands, then put it up to your chest. And when you bring it down, visualize that you bring down your heart with your hands.

We tell you something about your pain, my friends. Human beings do not learn through joy. They learn through turmoil, guilt, fear, and sadness. Some of the greatest lessons that have been accomplished by human souls have been because of those issues. But anyone who says to you, "Get rid of your pain. Let it go. Forget it. It was in the past," is not doing you a favor. Because you are in turmoil.

You need to understand that you need to honor that pain, be it a troubled childhood, be it a troubled marriage, low self-esteem, a death, any number of things that you have gone through in your lives. Each and every one of you will be different, but, please, you must honor this pain, for the lesson it has taught you, not for what it has felt like.

And until you can honor this pain and look into what it has taught you, you cannot let it go. It will not go away. You can stuff it down into the stomach area. You can stuff it down into the heart area or to the back of the head, and then you will have diseases of that nature in those positions.

And so we ask you to take your stone down from your chest and then look at it. You need to thank your heart for all the value that it has given you. It has kept you going when nothing else has. So, indeed, honor your heart for the goodness that it has and has given to you. Thank it for being there. Thank it for continually running when you have filled your entire body with corruption, pollution, junk.

And then look at that heart area, that beautiful pink stone of yours that has become your heart. Visualize a gray smudge as if it is a piece of dirt on that area and you need to ask out loud, "What is that smudge on my heart?" And you will immediately get an answer.

For some it might be, let us say, abuse. Child abuse would be a good example. You need to ask that heart of yours what you have learned from this issue. And you need to speak out loud so that the human mind will hear. Let us say, with this child abuse, you may have learned patience, courage, tears, standing on your own two feet, strength, acceptance, anger. There are many issues with child abuse and as in any of your other issues; there are many lessons. We ask you to say out loud, "Do I wish to let go of this issue and this lesson?"

There are some of you who will choose not to, my friends, because you have not learned totally all that you need to learn from that issue, whatever the issue it is. But, if you choose to let go of this issue from heart, you might rub that stone and you'll begin to feel a greasy or filmy texture upon the fingers. And when you feel that it is clean enough, you say out loud, "I thank you for the lessons that you have taught me, but I no longer need this lesson, and I wish to let it become more positive."

And then you let go of your hands and shake your hands to Mother Earth, and you ask that something beautiful be made from this energy, something positive, be it a tree, be it a flower, be it a plant or even a weed. Something that can give pleasure. And you must shake your hands very strongly indeed. When this is done, we ask you to go back to your heart and thank it once again, for you humans do much to your hearts that is rather negative.

And we ask you to put your hands as if in prayer and place them back into your chest. And then to go about your business. It can be done quite fast, my friends, but there needs to be a cleansing of the foundations of humanness. If there is not, you cannot go on to another doorway in growth. Many of you think that you have fixed your heart, your minds, your life. But if this were the case, you would not have disease. All disease is contributed to stress, but it is because you do not let it go. You hold on to it as if it is a valuable rarity, a gold coin, if you will.

And so, until you honor what it has taught you, you cannot let go of it. And this must be done in the next two to five years. If it is not done so, then you will continue in chaos. If it is done, you will be graduated.

J: How often do we do this practice?

G: As much as you feel the need. There are some who will be extreme in their nature who will choose to do this once, twice, three times a day. There will be some who choose to try it once a week and there'll be some who can only handle the intenseness of this exercise maybe once a month.

But, honor yourself, my friends, and give yourself permission to heal. You are the only ones who can do so. Your psychiatrists, teachers, ministers, psychics, your plain old people cannot do so. They cannot give you permission to heal until you give yourself permission to heal and until you honor what you have learned. That is the true way to let go of episodes in your life. Otherwise, you just put them back into the body, and they form into festering disease.

J: Why is it important that we do this now?

G: Because you are headed for an awakening. Your earth plane is headed for a gigantic awakening. There will be much chaos in the years to come, much fear, and those of you who are teachers need to be cleansed so that you have no fear. And so that you might help humanity come to where it needs to be. You are beginning to learn in a positive light. It is hard, we know this, but there need to be many teachers who can accomplish what has not been accomplished. And so that's why it needs to be done.

And those of you who wish to teach this example, those of you who wish to spread that idea, can do nothing but have more joy and more humans to help in the process. It is not a secret. It is not something that should be held to the heart. It is something that should be told about again and again and again so that more and more of you who wish to have a choice can do so.

When you have not cleansed the heart, there is a tendency for fear to come through the whole body. But when you have cleansed the heart, and you live in the vibration of joy, then there is not really any room for fear, but a moment in time. And that is the difference.

If you have a great deal of fear, if your heart has not been cleansed of the fear and pain, then it will just multiply. The fear will expand, and the more things happen to your earth, the more fear you bring about. Let us ask, how much fear was there at the time of your last earthquake?

J: Oh, lots.

G: Was it not expanded from one city, one place to many others? And indeed, why? There are many places where there will not be an earthquake, but fear was still there. It expanded. Let us ask you this. If you had an idea that nothing could come to you but joy and contentment and that there was no such thing as death and there was no ending, could you not expand that also? Would that not be the better?

And let us ask you this. If you were in the middle of that earthquake, and you reacted to that earthquake as if it were another incident, and you could be able to help others in need, would that not be felt?

And so that is the purpose of these lessons. In order to expand that which you call positive, you need to have the energy to do so. The energy of compassion and love is a great deal harder to get into the heart when there is so much muck than would be hate and envy and greed. That which you call positive is much harder to obtain and to keep. It is somehow more illusive in the human form than is the negative. It is easier to be in the negative than it is to be in the positive.

J: That's why so many people are into the negative.

G: Indeed, but the reason being is that you have so much negative in the heart already. So it is an easy matter to gain a little more. Do you not understand why it is so illusive, this joy that many of you hold?

J: Why is that?

G: Because there is a tendency not to be able to feel it.

J: That's true. We're so numbed out and dysfunctional.

G: Indeed, but that is because there is so much pain within each and everyone's heart that there is no room to feel the joy.

J: So we've got to get rid of that pain in order to replace it with joy and love.

G: Indeed so.

J: Because joy is the natural emotion of love.

G: Indeed so, and it will become the natural function.

Allowing

Part of the process for creating a new perspective for a more harmonious future is to learn to accept personal responsibil-

Healing the Human Spirit

ity for everything that shows up in our lives. Some of us blame all of our problems on something outside ourselves: our spouses, our jobs, the devil, the universe. But the angels, working psychologists that they are, recognize that our needs drive us to denial, over-indulgence, ego trips, and self-destruction. The answer is to accept and allow everything into our lives: the good, the bad, and the ugly. Once we allow, then we can face everything head-on instead of developing defense mechanisms to avoid them.

Allowing can begin as a ritual.

I: All you have to do is allow. Put your hands out, open them wide, and put your hands towards the heavens and allow.

How many humans have you seen who immediately cross their chest when they speak to another soul? This is closure. How many have you seen in recent history who have opened their hands up? This is the beginning.

We do not say it is a simple thing. We do not say that to open your hands and your heart is the cure all because every time a human being does this, a human being begins to fear. And they again begin to close up.

So every single day of your life say, "I allow all that is to come to me. I allow." And allow everything, all the goodness to come to you. "I allow all of the good of the universe to come to me. I allow." But you must open your hands. Do you really think that human beings do not have a technique for closure?

J: What do you mean by that?

I: Human beings are terrified of any experiences not of the norm. They are terrified of anything coming into their space. And so they close themselves up like tight little buds. How many people again have you seen in your recent history that will open themselves to others? Most human beings immediately expect that the most negative, worst part of emotion will come through to them. Because they do not feel worthy of being loved or admired or liked. And when you come to our side, when you wish to allow, how do you allow our side to come to you? Do you do so with closure? Or intellect? Or do you open your arms?

Now there are many souls who will attempt this. And they will open their arms and say, "I allow," and they will experience only those positive experiences to come in. They will want only those that they expect to come in.

Let us say you choose to see only an angel. When you put restrictions on allowing, you truly do not allow. When you say, "I wish to have an experience with money and it must be positive," then you are in reality saying, "I do not allow." When you say "I wish to experience the other side, but only the angels," then you are disallowing already. When you put limitations on experience, you are closing, you understand?

J: So, you have to be open to all of it.

I: You'll be open to all of it, but you can protect yourself. You can acknowledge that there are forces that are not always positive. You do not have to mix in with them, but you must allow them. "This is where you are, and I allow."

J: In other words, you acknowledge that they exist and you're not discounting or denying them, but you're choosing at this time to have a different experience.

I: Indeed. And those forces who are self-destructive, let us say other human beings, you might be on the side of their path. You might say to them, "Here's my hand, but if you choose not to take my hand, I allow." This is the hardest thing for parents to do. They tend to disallow human experiences with their children.

J: Yeah. We want to be protective and not have them experience anything bad.

I: Does that not put limitations on growth? And this is why we say that if you choose to go forward, if you choose to grow and to progress, you need to say, "I allow," and stop there.

We say to you: Touch not the emotions of others but live in thy own serenity. Which means you can allow the emotions of others, but you do not have to mix into them. You might live in your own serenity. When all around you is chaos, you can be an island of hope.

J: I guess that's what people are looking for so much now— that sense of empowerment, that they are in charge of their destiny, and that they can change it at any given time.

I: ***We'll tell you a secret.*** Most people who want to be in charge of their destiny also want to be in charge of others' destinies.

Let us ask you this question. You have begun, of late, to be very allowing, and you have begun to experience a lot of positivity in your growth. But how much do you worry about your child?

J: Oh, I guess it never stops.

I: How much do you worry about your mate?

J: Same thing.

I: Are you allowing? Or are you putting limitations that there can only be positivity in this relationship? "I will not allow anything else." You see, by saying that, you allow your own fears to come in.

Now, if you were to say, I allow whatever in this relationship or these relationships, and if you do not touch upon the other's path of fear or of any type of negative experience, you are not touched by it. And that's what humans must learn to do

J: It's hard to do.

I: It's called non-judgment. Are there not days that you have had recently where everything is really a gray area in your life and yet you have so much joy. The sun is out, the birds are singing, there's so much beauty, you just feel full of life and joy? And yet you have experiences in your life force that can be very negative, do you not?

J: That just happened today.

I: Again, it is allowing. It is saying: I will not have to touch the emotions of negativity. I will allow, but they do not come into me. You do not need to blend with those forces, but you can allow. This is what we are speaking of.

And when you begin to do this, when you begin to allow that great joy to come in, even though all around you in your life there is much negativity, that great joy comes in more and more.

J: I'm relating this right now to my openness to cultural diversity. Because of a video I'm producing, I was at an Islamic mosque today and a couple weeks ago at a Hindu temple. So I'm just experiencing more cultures and different ways that people see things. And now I'm at the point where I try to see out of their eyes. I try to walk in their shoes. I try to feel what it's like to be them and then experience it, acknowledge it, step out of it and return to myself. And now I have a new appreciation for them, although I may not want to believe what they do.

I: But you also have a great deal of joy, do you not?

J: Yes, I felt so joyful today.

I: Indeed. You might be joyful to be in a country that has no limitations or very little limitations on its female energies, but there is still joy. What you did is you opened your arms wide and you said, "I allow." And not one part of the experience touched you but joy. And that is what humans must do.

It is an illusive thing that they look for, but it is there. And all of you experience it at certain times in your life. And if you can learn how to do that when there is utter chaos totally around you, but you can still feel joy in the beauty of a morning or the song of a bird, then that is allowing. The great secret is to not put limitations on growth. And because human beings learn in disaster, that is how you grow.

J: Can't we change that?

I: Indeed, you are. When you can learn to have joy in the smallest thing while there is utter chaos around you, that is how you are learning to change things.

J: Because I would like to learn through love and joy and not through pain and struggle.

I: If you begin each new day by feeling the joy that you feel today, it feels cozy, does it not?

J: Mmm-mmm. Very warm.

I: Indeed. If you can find something to make you feel like that each and every day, you will feel less chaos and that is how humans will begin to change.

J: Well, we certainly do need to be accepting and tolerant of one another. That's a step in the right direction.

I: Why? Those are words that you use for emotions that are negative. You need to be more allowing. That is all. Tolerant is saying to another person: You're doing a very bad job at this, but it's all right, you're growing.

Again, touch not the emotions of others. Live in thy own serenity. This is what we're saying. And when all around you, you can feel joy when there is chaos, then you have succeeded in learning a great secret, and you will begin to teach it to others. When all around you is chaos and you can feel joy, **that is the secret.**

We do not mean that you cannot say, "This is wrong." It is wrong to kill other human beings. It is wrong to have pollutants in a society where they are available to small children. You must get in touch with your own realities because you humans have made it this way. But if you, again, can feel joy and allow even one person a day his or her own feelings, his or her own joy and sorrow and not try to touch on it, but just to allow, then you will be learning the secret.

J: But that's hard because we've been programmed to be of service to others and to "fix them" or help them or cure them, you know, like doctors.

I: There's a great difference in being of service to others and fixing them. You see, most human beings are not of service to others. They are trying to fix them because in their judgment, something is very wrong with them.'

J: But if we see someone doing something that we think could be done in a better way, don't we have the obligation to point that out?

I: That is not so. You have the choice. No one has an obligation.

J: But let's say I'm teaching students to type and they're doing something that needs correction, isn't that my responsibility, as a teacher, to correct that?

I: You are trying very hard not to say obligation, we realize that. That is the choice you have made, you understand, to be a teacher. But it is the way most human beings make choices that cause the problems, that cause the hurt. If someone was typing a letter and it was full of mistakes, you might say to that person, "You have very nice abilities. I've got this wonderful dictionary. Would you like to use mine? It's an interesting book."

J: That's subtle. (laughs)

I: Indeed. But there is also a need to allow each and every person to make his or her own choices. And you might say to that person, "I have a wonderful dictionary. If you cannot spell some of the words, would you like to use mine?" And then you need to allow that person to make his or her choice. And if they choose to get a "D" or an "F" instead of an "A" or a "B"—that must be their choice.

J: So, we teachers need to take on a totally different way of facilitating learning.

I: Why do you think you're schooling system is in such a mess? We would say to you that most teachers are in denial, that most teachers are afraid of being put out of their jobs, that most teachers choose to play along with a system they do not believe in. Out of fear. It has nothing to do with choices. When you have fear of an experience, you take away your choices.

That is why there are many like you who are needing to be in the background at this time for when that system begins to fail—and it will fail in a very big way—there needs to be many of you who can learn to do it differently. You see, most human beings tend to feel that they have obligations. That is not so. They have choices they make for other reasons than having to. So you must look at the choices that you make and find out why you make them.

J: Because by being introspective and looking at those choices, then we can choose to go in the accelerated way that you talked about before or choose to do something else.

I: When you make choices, you choose to grow in different aspects. You grow in different ways. You either grow into the negative as you call it, or into the positive.

J: But, if we get to the point where there is no such thing as negative or positive, there just "is," then we just grow.

I: Indeed. But are you to that point yet as humans? You see, on our side, we are at that point. On our side, we allow those of you we guard or teach or guide to make your own choices. It is you who choose to grow the way you wish to grow. And at some point in the next ten years, there will be a great upheaval of your society as you know it because a great many choices have been made for the negative. Again, it must swing back and balance to the positive. It cannot do so unless you make changes.

Energy Shields

Sometimes it becomes necessary to protect ourselves from unwanted negative forces in the world. Isabelle offered a new shielding technique for us to try.

I: We would like to tell you a new form of shielding your-self and giving yourself extra energy. Close your eyes and see a favorite color or a color of spirituality right in front of your face in vibrant color, big and circular. Have you picked a color?

We ask you to take a deep breath through the nostrils and inhale that color right into your whole body. Take a very deep breath. And then when you begin to exhale, exhale the color out through each and every pore of your being.

Do it two more times, with separate colors. The same thing. Do you see another color out in front of you? And as you inhale, it becomes a vapor-like color and goes into the body. As you exhale, it comes out through each and every pore. And as it comes out, it begins to form a shield around you, each and every color, approximately ten feet out...shimmering and beautiful. And each suc-cessive color will be further out. And you do this three times with three different colors.

J: So I do, for example, three blue, then three yellow, and three green?

I: No, we ask you to do one of each. Three times. But you might feel the need to be protected even more and so if you do feel the need to be protected, you might do as you wish.

J: Does it matter which colors you choose?

I: Ask for a protective color. It will come. Try so now please. Let us say, you were to see a protective color of purple. Breathe that color in through the nostrils and hold it for a few seconds and then force it out each and every pore of your being, and as you do, it goes out into the ethers about ten feet, you see? And you begin to have a very wonderful shield. This is something that many of you must do in the coming months. It is a way for you to protect yourselves even more than you usually do. It is also a way to get much more energy and to feel lighter.

But they must be your own colors. Please do not suggest a color to yourself. Just ask and you will find it. And they will be different at all times.

This might be very interesting as an experiment for you all to try. It is something that must be accomplished by each and every one to his or her own satisfaction. But when you are done, you'll have an aura or a shield that is approximately ten to twelve feet out from you on all sides, and it will be encompassing you with all these protective colors. And they will be your very own shield, not everyone else's.

So this might help. We ask you to tell this one (Rosie) that, so that she can get some help, also.

J: Yes, I will. What does it protect us from, exactly?

I: In the coming months and years even, there is going to be much chaos on your planet, much havoc, and you will need to shield yourself from those people who have so much fear that they cannot think without taking other's energies, and also from things that you choose not to be hurt by. It is something that all of you on the path need to do as a way of protection against havoc and chaos. There will be a great deal of it in the coming seven years.

But in the next few months, many people will be having a lesson in truth, meaning that your greatest fears will be realized. You'll be able to understand that which you fear. You will be given a tool for letting go of those fears, but many of you will not understand this and will become chaotic in your thinking. It is something that will be happening. We choose to help as many as possible, but many will not listen. And so we need to warn those others who choose to listen to protect themselves as strongly as possible. This is a new way of protection that is coming into being with the new chakra that you humans are beginning to talk about.

J: What's the new chakra?

I: It is the chakra of telling truth as you see it, and it is formed on the side of your neck. Towards your throat, your esophagus, you know where you speak from? And it is the color of teal.

That is why so much of that color has come into being in the last year or so. It is a different color for a different dimension.

But many of you who begin to wear this color, who see it in many places and love this color, will begin to find yourselves in a bit of trouble at times because you will stick your foot into your mouth and chew thoroughly.

It is a way of you telling truth that makes you feel cleansed. And so many of you are afraid of this and will feel that you are in trouble for the most part. But it is something that needs to be done. Again, it is foundation cleansing. It is a way of letting go of those fears by telling or speaking your own truth.

But this also is an exercise in protection and it goes along with this new chakra. You may feel much lighter when you do this. You may feel much happier and much more satisfied in your day when you do this. If you do this before you begin your day, you might feel much lighter and happier, and also we suggest you do this at night.

J: So just ask for three colors?

I: Ask for them to be shown to you. Let us do an experiment at this time. Close your eyes, please, and ask for a color out loud.

J: All right. I ask for a color of protection.

I: And what do you get?

J: A rose color.

I: Indeed. And so, somewhat of a magenta, is it not? That is what we have given you. So you breathe that in, and it is as if it becomes a vapor. And you breathe it in through your nose, and you hold it for a few seconds and through your body, your entire body, and then you force out the breath and that color goes out into each and every pore and out into the ethers, and you will begin to see it around your body. It is further out than most people do their protection color.

And you do this two other times and then you ask for another color. Let us try this.

J: All right. I ask for another color of protection.

I: And your color?

J: It just seems either green or blue.

I: It is a blue color. It is interesting that you said that because we were thinking of teal, which is a blue-green color, but then we decided to give you a blue.
So, take the deep breath through the nostrils and have it go out through each pore of the body. And as you feel it coming through the pores, it becomes a beautiful color out, a shimmering arc of light, around your body. And you might do this once more, please.

J: I ask for a third color of protection.

I: And your color?

J: I'm thinking green, but not seeing it.

I: Think again. Ask again.

J: Okay. Please show me another color. Oh, I don't know, it looks orange to me.

I: Indeed. And so you do this one more time. Now begin to see yourself with these arcs of color, or light as you call them, shimmering about you, approximately ten feet out. Now, how do you feel?

J: I feel lighter.

I: Indeed, you will, and this is something that you must begin to do. We tell you one thing that is interesting. As more and more people become sensitives, and they begin to roam at night, those people in havoc may choose to try to partake of other's energies. And so this would be a very good thing to do at night, also.

And it is something that is quite interesting that, at various times of your day and in different times of your life, you will find different colors needed and accept what is given. And if you cannot see it, my friend, feel it. And this will help many souls. It is a new technique that we are giving you today, and all of you will feel lighter and be much more abundant in energy.

As your country and your world go through transition, and as you know, it is going very fast indeed into different levels of thinking, philosophies and even dimensions, there are many souls upon your planet who are in a great deal of chaos and into chaotic thinking. During the next two-year period, every single person on your earth plane will be given the chance to view his or her greatest fears. He or she will also be given a chance to start to work with those fears so that he or she can be rid of them.

Some souls fear rejection. Some souls are insecure. Some souls fear having communication with others. Whatever your fear may be, you will be given an opportunity in the next two years to dwell on it, think about it and resolve it. You will be given tools to do this. It is highly important that you begin to use those tools. Now most of you would be willing to say that you cannot understand tools, but it will come to each and every one of you.

Because of the atmospheric and chaotic conditions on your planet at this time, there is great chaos on your planet and even above your planet.

J: What do you mean by above our planet?

I: We mean to say to you that there are pulls from other stars, other atmospheres, other gravities, and other planets, that are affecting your planet. They affect your earth changes, even your weather. A great many other changes are in store for your planet. But the reason you need to protect yourself with these three colors now is that many of your souls will be leaving their bodies at this time. We do not say all will be in death. We say to you that many of you are becoming more sensitive and more in tune with your talents. And you choose to begin to go out of body especially during sleep.

Now many of these souls who are in chaos find themselves in much difficulty with their energy. And so there must be a way to gain extra energy. So those who are in spiritual development need to be protected from energy grabbers. Those souls who choose to come out of their body during sleep tend to look for energy wherever and whenever they can receive it. Some of these souls do not know how to go about getting their own energy replaced. And so you will find yourselves at times awakening in the morning hours very tired and very low in energy.

That is why you need to protect yourself at night at this time. It is not something that is so horrible or frightening. It is just a fact of life at this time. Where there is chaos, there is energy depletion.

And so, if you protect yourself as you go to sleep and when you rise in the morning, you will be much more energetic and also you will be fed extra energy from your guides and your guardians.

Calling Upon Past Life Experiences

Another technique to help heal our spirit and enhance our self-esteem is to learn to call upon past life experiences to guide us through our present life. For example, Isaac Asimov, the amazing author of 467 books, not only called upon his experience and knowledge from his former lives to write all of his books, but he tapped into other people's lives as well.

I: *We will tell you another secret.* There is not a person on your earth who does not use experiences from other lifetimes in order to do things. As you have been a mother, there are many lifetimes when you experienced motherhood. Some of you say that it is instinctive to be a mother, but this is not the case. Here are many souls who choose to do things over and over as a way of expressing themselves. Whether you call that genius or not is in your own thinking pattern. But there is not a single soul on your earth who does not use a great many of their past life experiences from each and every lifetime to learn.

J: Now, as an educator, how can I help my students tap into their own genius? What could I do to facilitate that?

I: It would be wonderful if you could use meditation. It would be wonderful if you could get them to think inside of themselves. It would be wonderful to visualize...let us say to you, if you wish to learn to play the violin, you could tap into that energy to see if you've had a lifetime to play the violin. And you could visualize yourself in that lifetime playing the violin.

It would be very interesting to see what happens with this basically because there are some souls who have the abilities to tap into other people's lifetimes. Why do you think Isaac Asimov is so prolific? Do you really think that he does not tap into some other energies?

J: He must have.

I: He has done so, but this is without his knowledge. Basically, that again is a personality who is trying to balance left and right brain, but leans towards the left.

So it would be very interesting to see some of your pupils who choose to tap into any lifetime where the violin was being played. You might be very surprised at what you would get.

J: Okay, I'm trying to play golf and I can visualize myself somewhere in the future being this golf pro, and I can tap into that or maybe somebody else?

I: You can even do so in the past. Who is your most famous golfer?

J: Probably Jack Nicklaus.

I: Could you not visualize yourself tapping into his past in this lifetime and learning how to play golf as Jack Nicklaus? You might be very surprised with what you get.

J: I'm gonna try that. (laughs) Next time I'm at the golf course.

I: Why not try it in your arm chair? The past that you tap into, that you walk into, that body of that past—you become that person. You might be very surprised at what you receive.

J: You could really do that with anybody that you want to identify with then.

I: Indeed, you can.

J: I'm thinking of, like, Mother Teresa, people I admire.

I: We ask you a question. Again, human beings tend to be so negative. Why do your children have these murderous sprees and say that they have been influenced by certain murderers or serial killers? It is because they tap into their body, into that memory, and they wish to be like that personality. So they become like that personality. Do you think they were always that way? It is that they tap into that energy.

And it is much easier to deal with the negative type of energy. Again, once the energy begins, it is always there. Once the energy of a soul is, it is always there. Once the life of one of those souls is, it is always there. It never leaves. It is there as energy.

J: And we have access to their energy?

I: Indeed, you do.

J: Okay. So, I admire the writer Kahlil Gibran, and if I wanted to tap into his experience and wisdom, I would just visualize myself as him?

I: We have a treat for you. We wish you to do an experiment. We wish you to take your favorite poem from that personality.

J: Well, I don't remember it precisely, but it's something about parents treating their children like arrows and letting them go.

I: All right. We wish you to find that passage in a book. We wish you to read it out loud, and then we wish you to sit quietly and go out of body, because that is what you do when you meditate. We wish you to visualize yourself writing that poem in his body. And we wish you to visualize how it felt to put those words down as that soul. And then you might come back and try it with your own poetry.

There is energy that you can tap into from hundreds and hundreds and thousands of years ago. It is up to you to learn how to use it. It is there for the partaking, but you seem to not know. There is a group of your people who do their running and jumping every few years?

J: Oh, the Olympics.

I: Yes. Do you know that there is a process that some of those human beings are using even now to tap into the energy? They visualize themselves winning and having won the race. That is part of what we are speaking of.

When you allow that energy to come into being, it is always there. That is why so many of your ghosts are pure energy. They are memories that have been trapped in time. It is not that they are poor, sorrowful souls that are trapped. A great many of your so-called ghosts are energy and memories, and you can remove that energy and make it into something else.

J: But then would you be able to tap into it safely, to glean some genius from it or wisdom from it?

I: If you try, indeed. But you must be very sure what you want to tap into.

J: Yeah, it could be scary, huh?

I: Again, some of your youngsters today tap into energy. There is one that you have had much trouble with in the past. His name is Charles Manson. A great many of your children are tapping into that energy. Why do you think so many revere that soul?

It is very easy to tap into the negative, especially if you wish to have some sort of power over another. But it is much more interesting to tap into the positive, is it not? So why not tap into one of the most beautiful opera singers or a great violinist or a writer or a scientist?

It is not easy to do this. We tell you this. You might have to try three, four or five, even ten times. But it is an interesting experience, and it can be very enlightening and delightful.

So become your Mr. Nicklaus. And see what it feels like to hit one of those balls in one of...we find this interesting because it really is not a hole.

J: Oh, it's a cup, yeah, it's a little....

I: A little cave, if you will. Challenging, to say the least.

Contacting Our Angels

We can never underestimate the healing power of our guardian angels. They, who have known us intimately since birth, offer comfort and warmth when we learn how to contact them.

I: If you have the ability to be quiet inside, to still yourself, and if you have the desire to listen and to not put judgment onto what you hear, then you can hear from our side. Many of you choose to think that those words that they hear in their heads have a tendency to be "mind chatter."

It is only when certain people have experiences with angels out of fear—let us say, an angel warns a person of an accident about to happen—that most of you choose to listen to us.

Now we suggest to you that you surround yourself with light and that you use the protective colors that Gabriel has given you. And then find a place to sit quietly. You might have a desire to ask questions of your angel, or you might want to hear his or her name. You see, most of our form do not have male/female characteristics. It is what each and everyone of you choose to deal with in your own minds. We again comply and become what it is you wish to feel comfortable and safe with.

Some of you wish to have very stern advisors. Some of you wish to have advisors who are very soft and caring and gentle. Some of you wish to have happy and carefree type of sprites. And we comply with all of these if you wish.

We do say to you that you'll be given a name that will make you feel comfortable with your angel. Then you might begin by asking questions. As you still yourself within, you'll begin to hear answers and what you must do is learn to differentiate between the sound of the voice on our side and the sound of the voice in your head. And it will come about if you keep trying. There is not one of us who has not tried to give you answers, and guide, help, and love you, and for the most part, most of you choose not to listen. It is only when you have great fear or great consternation that you open up the telephone.

And so we wait and comply with what is needed. And we keep trying to reach each and every one of you. There are many things in your life that most of you choose not to see. Many spirits have contacted your earth plane from our world, from other worlds, and most human beings choose not to see these. They have a great deal of fear of something that they cannot understand logically. And so it is a time period of great chaos in the mind, also. Not only is your world in a great deal of chaos, so are all of your minds, and when you begin to open up, there is a tendency for you to think that you're going crazy or that you are having delusions.

There are even some souls who choose to say that anyone who hears an angel or a guide is under the power of your evil ones. This is not true, my friend. If you ask for higher beings and you ask to be protected from anything that is negative or that is confused, then you will get higher beings. What you ask for is what you normally get.

We do say that there are entities about who are confused. There is a great deal of energy that is turned into the negative, that you can say are demons. But, in each and every case, there is a human being present manifesting fear.

And that is one thing that we find interesting about human beings. When they begin to fear something such as the unknown, they begin to enlarge on that fear, and they begin to manifest more and more and more. And as they manifest more, the energy becomes larger. And they find themselves in a dither of confusion and fear. We say to you that, yes, there are in your world energies that you consider demonic, but in every case there is a human being unleashing that energy.

J: Is the human being causing it?

I: The human being is like a conductor. The human being, yes, indeed, brings it about by manifesting it in the first place.

How many of you choose to believe in anything that has been what we term mystical, such as angels? Even now, in your country, there are only approximately 70% of people who choose to believe in angels, and yet we exist.

But when more and more of your people begin to allow the energy to be manifested in a way that is positive and that can be conducive to our energy, then we begin to become more like a normal thought process. We become manifested in your earth plane because we are allowed to become a part of your earth.

There is something interesting about people that you call angels or guides or mentors. Those of the higher natures choose not to become involved unless asked.

On the other hand, there is negativity about, and it can become quite an interesting phenomena with human beings manifesting that more and more.

It is even something that most human beings would not even think of, that they can begin to manifest those things they fear the most just by worrying about them or having fear about them. And then they become manifested, indeed. They become great and strong and the only thing that you can do when you have that problem is to begin to turn the tide by manifesting the positive.

J: And if we start manifesting the positive, will we begin to see angels more in our lives? Haven't they appeared in our past?

I: When there are special cases, when there is need for your history.

Again, it is because humans need these stories and legends in order to go on. Let us take someone who has allowed the negative to become very grand, indeed, and has allowed satanic or demonic forces into his or her life. Isn't it an interesting thing that you can have another person come to your rescue, say, a priest or minister and that person, by just shouting and being very confident in himself, can destroy that demonic force? So again, it is the positive that brings the positive. It is the negative that brings the negative.

And there are many of your souls who choose to say that they are positive thinkers. In reality they are in denial. They choose not to think about anything if it has any form of negativity, but that is also a fear, my friend. And these people do not understand that, when they feel like they are manifesting or saying affirmations, these things will come about for them. And when they do not, it just throws them into a tizzy.

When you believe truly that things are good, that people are kind, that your life is rainbows, then you will still have problems, but it will not be so hard for you. It will not be so stressful for you. And you will find a lot more positivity in your life than negativity. And we think this is something that each and every human being must learn before too long.

Increasing Our Self-Esteem

Before we can accept and appreciate the goodness in others, we must first see it in ourselves. When we increase our level of self-esteem, we are in a far better position to help others in a non-enabling way.

I: Any person who enables has a lower self-esteem. And if you are going to truly help your fellow man, you need to feel good about yourself so that you can do it in a positive way.

This is going to be the hardest lesson that any of you will ever have to learn upon your planet. To have a good feeling about self is almost an impossibility with human beings. We do not understand this, but it is so. If you can begin to think of yourself as a piece of the whole, as a spark of the Creator, as a being made in the image of All, then you might begin to say to yourself, "Is this a good thing that I destroy a piece of the God?"

There are many ways that human beings destroy themselves, you know? It is not only through alcohol, drugs, food, or any other of your wonderful addictions. We say "wonderful" addictions because they do teach you something, do they not?

You must begin to look at yourselves and see the beauty that lies therein, and we do not mean facial beauty, nor inner beauty even. We mean that if you can see yourself as a part of the whole, if you can see yourself as a part of a light, you might be much more interested in making that light shine.

J: Yes. If we can see the divine in ourselves and in others. But there are so many people out there who want to put human beings down and say "human beings are nothing, God is everything," but they don't realize that we're connected to God, we're part of God.

I: Indeed, the Creator is everything. But then you are a part of everything, are you not? You are a part of your fellow man. You are a part of your trees, your birds, your animals, and your oceans. You are a part of your sky and your clouds. And if you are a part of the everything, should not you honor everything?

The thing that fascinates us on this side is that you might honor a great many things, but very few of you honor yourselves.

J: That's true. Or our planet.

I: Indeed. And a great deal of you do things that are just thoughtless. It's not that you do things to be destructive.

It is that you do things because you are too involved with your time or with what others think. You are too involved in fear. Most human beings who do destructive things do so because they are thoughtless.

It is always hurry, hurry, hurry, and then you cannot stop and see that you are thoughtless or self-destructive or even destructive to other things. Maybe if you all threw your clocks away, you might have a more interesting time.

J: (laughs) I agree with that. Other countries really have a slower way of operating. Like in Mexico, they take siestas. I've always felt that the way we live our lives in the United States is much too rushed.

I: Indeed, it is. It's much too stress-filled, also.

But almost all of the destruction on your earth plane is through thoughtlessness. If you became aware, if you could feel what a tree feels like to not have water, if you could feel what a little animal feels like not to be touched, to be ignored, to be fed only at certain times, to be at the mercy of someone who might be thoughtless, if you could feel what other people feel when you say a thoughtless word, you might be very surprised at how soon your world will turn around.

We suggest a nice little exercise for you the next time you find yourself doing something thoughtless. All of you recognize the thoughtlessness that you do right after you do it, so if you could recognize that and turn it around and think to yourself, how did that other person, that animal, that ground, how did all these things feel when I did my thoughtless act? Take the time to analyze it, and you'll begin to see a change.

Now we think it's very interesting in your Depression in the 1930s, most of you had to learn to take the time to make little things a pleasure. Most of you had to learn to make do. And most of you were better for it.

And so that is one reason why your planet is in so much chaos because you have so many people who are thoughtless in your deeds and do not want to pay for the thoughtlessness. And there is always a time when you shall have to pay.

Using The Dream State

The great genius, Albert Einstein, said that his theory of relativity came to him while he was dreaming. Like him, we can tap into help from the other side while we sleep.

D: A great many of your wonderful inventions and thought processes are in dream states, and it is always a matter of someone helping from this side. Always. For that is when you are most open.

J: So all those people on this plane who want to be inventors or who come up with new ways of thinking should just ask in their dream state to be led?

D: Tell them to open their ears and their minds. Tell them to stop feeling limited. A good way to stop feeling limited is to ask for help. A great many of your souls find that very hard to do. If you wish to really achieve, open up the minds, open up the heart, and allow. Ask for help.

We say to you also that too many of you ask for help, and you do not take it in. You do not receive it. You put up a block.

J: Is it because we don't recognize it, or do we just resist it?

D: It is due to your level of pride. It is very hard for the human being to accept help. In fact, for some, it may be impossible. Because of that one little word, pride.

J: But, when we can break down that barrier, we can start connecting to those voices and get help from the other side?

D: Indeed. And it is also a way of limiting yourself when you use that word, pride.

J: Well, you know that saying, pride goeth before a fall.

D: We were saying that to you in your mind. Did you know this?

J: No.

D: Do you see what we say about humans listening?

J: That came from your side?

D: Indeed, it did.

Another positive outcome of the dream state is that it allows us to see inside ourselves so that we might become more whole through introspection. Isabelle helped explain the meaning of a bad dream which Jennifer had experienced.

J: I had a terrible dream last night.

I: Could we help with this please?

J: I am in someone's home asleep, and I wake up to a party that some of my former students are having. And I realize that my purse is near them, and they had taken my wallet and credit cards. I ask them to put the wallet back, but they leave instead. I realize my wallet is ripped, and the money is gone. So I go to my childhood home to see if anything else is missing. When I look in my bedroom, everything is there except the mirror on the wall. So then I flip off the light, and I start to go down the hallway to see my parents' room, but then something makes me want to go back and look one more time at my bedroom. I try the light. It doesn't work, and I think, "Well, maybe the light bulb burned out." So I try another switch. It doesn't work.

Then I realize somebody has turned off the fuses in the house. And I look up to see this big, tall, dark male figure coming down the hallway to get me. And then I scream, "No, no!" and I woke up.

I: We will speak to you on this if you will listen carefully. We say to you, my friend, that the purse and the wallet is your self, everything that you consider Jennifer Martin is made up of the purse and wallet. It is your identity.

Your credit cards, your money, your important papers, are all of your talents. All of the things that belong to you.

Your students have been very much in the past a group of souls who truly do not at times identify with you. They at times invalidate you and you feel this. And all those talents that you give to them are somehow at times abused or rejected.

And that is what that part of the dream is about. As you go back to your childhood home to find if something else was missing, you indeed found it. You found the mirror. Again, this is your identity. Your room was your identity. And when you did not see things in your room, you were invalidated. And that is why you went down to your parents' room.

Now your parents' room signifies that those are the souls who invalidated you. You have much more in common with your friend (Rosie) than you understand at this time. You, too, were invalidated in different ways. You, too, have become a non-person in different ways. And, if it was not for your talents, you would have lost yourself, too.

We say to you that the very large, dark man in the darkness are your greatest fears, that something reaching out to get you.

But it was again the fear of having something taken away from you. More of your talents. More of your traits. And also more invalidation.

And that is why there was darkness. When there is something that you fear, there is always darkness. It is because you do not see the light on the matter.

And as the big, dark person was coming from your parents', let us say, down the hall from your parents' room...

J: No, it was coming from the kitchen.

I: Okay. Let us ask you, who do you think invalidated you the most? Let us say, your mother. Where was your mother's domain?

J: Oh, the kitchen.

I: Now, we say to you...the more that you have not found work, the more that you have fears of finances, the more that you feel invalidated and your talents become invalidated, the more you have nightmares.

And what your dream was trying to represent is that your childhood was the beginning of the invalidation, and it has carried through into your teaching. Many of your students do not recognize your talent as such. They do not recognize your person. And they invalidate you. And that is what your purse represents, everything that is you. It is a holding apparatus. Just as the human body is a vehicle, so is the purse.

And this is your dream. Does this make sense to you?

J: It really does. It's just totally what's happening right now. So the dream was to call my attention to my fears and things that are bothering me.

I: It is also to call attention to where you are coming from, how you operate in an adult body in an adult world. You operate on the premise that you will be invalidated.

J: Yes. And that's stemming from childhood.

I: Indeed. And directly from your mother.

J: So how do you get rid of that?

I: You begin to acknowledge it and to see it for what it is. Our friend, Gabriel, has a wonderful technique of "I allow." And you know it will help you.

But because you are an intellectual personality, when you begin to see that which is, and it is masked in all these innuendos, you will be able to work on it at a much faster rate—when you begin to know that is what you are dealing with.

And so now you know. And we will say to you that when you begin to work, not on the problem, but on the solution, then you will fix it all.

And the problem you know. The solution is to allow, to begin to have self-love for yourself and for all.

Chapter 7

A New Perspective of the Past

Walk with your God, hold that soul's hand if you wish to use that as an analogy, but you cannot expect that any deity, be it Buddha, be it Jesus, be it the Source, or any other deity on your earth plane—and there are thousands of them—you cannot expect them to take responsibility for your lessons.

When Women Ruled

This planet has not only undergone tumultuous physical changes since its formation, but our socialization processes have dramatically transformed over the centuries.

J: My understanding is that for the past 3,000 years we've been socialized on this planet to serve in a male-dominant perspective civilization. Before this, the women were dominant, and so men kind of went overboard in trying to balance things, and now it's on the other side. It's almost like, the use of drugs—or as my friend Jane puts it—the toxic waste of youth, is a symptom of this imbalance which needs to be corrected. So, how do we go about correcting a male-dominant perspective civilization?

I: You are correct. At one point women had a great deal of power because they were considered the mothers of races. They were the life force, the life-givers for human beings. And so they did dominate. But humans must experience each polarity. And when it swung over to the dominance of males, your earth plane was experiencing the opposite polarity. And we need to tell you that there has been balance for thousands of years between the sexes, and you have experienced each side of the polarities, and now it is up to all of you to experience the middle.

Part of the problem is there are so many of you who have such anger with this subject and instead of allowing that each and every one is an important part of the whole, there is a tendency to want control and power over the opposite sex. And again the only way that you can rectify this problem, so you can begin to live in the balance of male and female energy, is to do it yourself one by one. When you no longer have to defend and yet do your work, do your life as you see fit, then you will have balance.

In each sex, there are souls who wish to control through anger. And they incite others to feel that way, too. Again, we tell you to touch not the emotions of others and that means that if you feel whole as a woman, as a human being, then you do not have to have the anger. And if you feel that there is injustice in the work market, then you yourself must speak up on this for yourself. And in doing so, you will help others.

J: But what about countries like India where they burn women whose dowries aren't enough or China where they kill little girls just because they are females? What do you do about that injustice?

I: What you do about those injustices is to touch not the emotions of those species. What you do is you show a mirror of what it could be like. Why do you think so many of your women are coming to this country from those very countries that do this to them? It is because they have seen a mirror of what it could be like.

And by your very deeds, by your very actions, things will begin to change in other parts of the world. But you cannot put your philosophy, your judgment onto other species, other countries. And so the only thing you can do is to change your world. And by changing your world, by changing the looks, the appearance, and the feelings of your world, then other parts of the world will swing into that thinking eventually.

There has been much progress in many of these countries that you speak of. But human beings are an impatient lot. They tend to want it to happen, oh, let us say, last year, you understand? And so there is a tendency for you not to see the goodness or the progress that has happened thus far.

So, we ask you to look upon the positive. Yes, there will always be a negativity in your world because of polarities. If you did not have any polarities, my friend, you would not have a way to learn. You would not have a school house on this plane. But we must say to you, glorify that heart of yours because it is a very special part of you. All will come in time.

Jesus Christ, the Bible, Miracles, and a Whole Lot of Other Things

With all that has been written, preached, and believed about Jesus of Nazareth, one significant aspect about him has never been mentioned: He was an angelic soul who took on human form to teach us an uncommon love.

I: He came to teach basically love. And your Bible and many of your fine folk have chosen to use his words in an intellectual capacity, to turn things to their way of thinking a great deal of the time. And you have to understand that though your Jesus, your Buddha, many of your other souls, were all very highly evolved entities; they were also human. And so they had the emotions of humans. Your Jesus was not all sugar and spice and light.

J: I've heard that he had a bad temper.

I: He had a great deal of anger at times, indeed. But we say to you, yes, he was the son of God. But then, so are you. It is just that those entities that you call Jesus and Buddha were expanded mightily compared to someone who has been around for a few thousand years.

J: Well, Jesus told us that he was not the exception, he was the example and that we could be just like him.

I: Just as your Hitler was the example. He was everything *not* to be, was he not?

J: Right.

I: Again, you see the polarities? And because human beings need those polarities desperately in order to experience, that is complied with. But as for beings of light and energy, yes, your Jesus was an expanded soul. But again, you can do the same.

J: Getting back to his temper for a bit, I just have to laugh because we have this sanctified image of him, you know, turning the other cheek, and being this soft, almost wimpy kind of personality, and I've never thought Jesus would have that kind of quality. I've always thought he was a charismatic leader and would exhibit exuberance and anger, all of it. My question is, why was he mad and could you elaborate on his other personality traits?

I: When you make the commitment to become human in any form, we do not care if it is a savior or a garbage man, you allow polarities. It is something that humans must experience. This is the way your earth plane has been constructed. This is how you learn great lessons.

So, why is it an interesting thing to find out that your Jesus had human reactions and human polarities? He was a personality who came with all the goods of humanness. And so he acted as a human would act. The reason your Jesus had a temper is because he chose to deal with injustice. And as a human, a natural reaction of injustice is anger, is it not? And that is why he chose to exhibit anger.

Let us tell you something very important. If your Jesus came to your earth plane as a higher soul or deity, whatever you wish to call it, but someone who was not what you humans think of as solid and definitely not human, do you think that he would really have gotten anywhere with any one of you?

J: (laughs) Not really.

I: Indeed. And especially in those times, but again in your times also, he would have been looked on with suspicion. He would have been looked on with distaste. He would have been looked on with fear. And he could not have done his work. And the interesting part of this is that human beings need to understand that you can also turn the other cheek, but you can fight injustice. You can do both at the same time. We say to you that when you speak of turning the other cheek, in reality that means that you do not have to have anger to acknowledge other people's negativity. Does that make sense to you?

J: Yes, it does.

I: People think that in your Bible that Jesus' saying of turning the other cheek is meaning to get hit on one side, then to turn the other cheek so you can get hit again. But this is not a proper analogy. It means that you can touch not the emotions of those who are negative. But you can be aware of them and you can deal with your own emotions in a more positive way, you understand?

J: Yes. Maybe just turn to a different perspective.

I: And we will say to you something important. Your Jesus did not turn the other cheek when there was injustice. What he was saying to you was to allow those feelings of others, not to touch them.

J: Yeah, you know, I was watching part of a Billy Graham program the other night, and I'm wondering what Jesus thinks about people who keep talking about surrendering their lives to him. They claim that Jesus came here to redeem their sins, and all they have to do is be baptized and they're saved from hell. What does Jesus think about all this?

I: That personality does not think about those things as that personality has gone into the blend. But we will say to you that it is not what he meant. You do not surrender your life to anyone but self. You can be with your God. You can blend with your God. You can understand your God, but you are here to create that which you desire. And we say to you that this is another way of putting blame on others, including your God, as a way of not putting blame on self.

And so those souls who choose to surrender to their deity or their Jesus are asking for a way out of their dilemmas, their education. And to say that we surrender to you and so you will take care of all of our sins is a way of saying, "We do not wish to take responsibility." Souls should not wish to let go of all responsibility. They should love their deities on a side-by-side basis. Walk with your God, hold that soul's hand if you wish to use that as an analogy, but you cannot expect that any deity, be it Buddha, be it Jesus, be it the Source, any other deity on your earth plane—and there are thousands of them—you cannot expect them to take responsibility for your lessons.

That is not why your Jesus came. Your Jesus came to the earth plane in order to make you more human, to understand more about what it feels like to be on this side. And so it is a very hard thing to say: "You take my sins. You be responsible for them." Because any deity that you wish to call on will not take that. Those souls who think that they have gotten out of their predicament will have a very interesting surprise when they come to our side, because it is still there.

J: But yet, you know, everybody thinks that they've got the only truth. I was at an Islamic celebration yesterday videotaping for a production at the college and in talking to the imam, their religious leader, he mentioned that Mohammed is the one, true and only prophet of God. And when you listen to Catholics, they say the Catholic church is the one true church and all the rest are wrong. Everybody thinks that they've got the one answer, that their religion is right and everybody else's is wrong.

I: Do you know why this is so? Because those souls who choose to express this opinion have a great fear down deep inside that what they wish so mightily for may not be the truth. When you say to another, "I am better than you because I have the one true God," you are basically saying, "I'm afraid that might not be so." And so this is a prejudicial thinking for many of you, and we say to you that any god, any deity, is what you need at that time.

What you call God, what you call the Force or the Source, is in fact a very impersonal force. That soul does not think in terms of being perfect. That being does not think in terms of right or wrong. That being does not think in terms of who knows me the best. And so it is a great deal of interest to us on this side to see how very prejudiced many of you are in your faith. That is not faith, my friend, that is fear. We will tell you that when you overcome fear of other religious philosophies and you can say, "If this interests you, then all is well," that is when you have true faith.

J: Yes. There are so many ways of looking at it, and any time you try to shove your perspective down someone else's throat, you're acknowledging that you doubt that yours is the right way.

I: Indeed. Anyone who is a power in any of your philosophies does this as a way of controlling others. It is a way of gathering people who fear that they have nothing in their hearts or souls to hang on to, and they can be empowered by all these little ones. And so when those souls say to you unequivocally that this is the only, true philosophy, and anybody else who does not think in our way is damned, this is a form of control. And it is not your God's control. It is human control.

J: I've always felt that about most churches, that they just kind of sold fire insurance. You know, you'll burn in hell if you don't believe what we say, and so it just sets out this fear, "Gee, I don't want to burn in hell, so I'll join this church."

I: We say to you, also, that there are many of your brothers and sisters who join churches as a way out of responsibility for their own actions and thinking processes. It is a wonderful way to deal with putting your actions under the carpet.

J: Yeah, they're so self-righteous. If anybody criticizes them or disagrees with them, they reply, "Oh, you're going to hell because it says so in the Bible," you know?

I: Your Bible has been prostituted so many times that the word of your savior cannot possibly have meaning, true meaning as it was meant to have for your people. It has been prostituted by those who choose to control and by those who have their own processes.

For example, when this book was beginning, your God did not choose to think of women as being the lesser. And you will notice that in your Bible, this is what happens. Your God chooses to think of each and every soul as an equal unto others. And there are no sexes in this side of thinking.

J: Will there be a second coming of Christ?

I: There already has been.

J: Can you tell us about it?

I: It is in each and every one of you. Have you not begun to recognize, my friend, that the Christ is within?

J: Yes. That is the second coming?

I: Indeed it is. It is hard for many of you to understand this. Just as so many of your souls choose to think that your extraterrestrials will come down and swoop you away from all this chaos and havoc, many souls on your planet choose to believe that another coming of the Jesus Christ personality will wipe away all of the chaos, anger, and negativity.

J: Right. That's their interpretation of the Bible.

I: Indeed it is, but we will tell you that in the first coming, it did not wipe away all the anger and chaos and negativity, did it?

J: No.

I: Your Jesus came to teach souls how to love in a gentle way. He came to teach souls how to control themselves and be responsible for their own actions. That is why he came. He did not come to absolve all sins. He did not come to make everything clear and clean again. He came to teach. He was a teacher. But most of you have to put a connotation on the idea that a Christ-like soul comes for anything besides absolving all mankind from all of their sins all of the time. It is a wonderful way to not be responsible for your own actions. And no matter how many times you ask for spiritual cleansing, no matter how many times you ask for the wiping away of sins even before death, when you get on our side, you have a big surprise waiting because you will still have to look at those things.

Jesus, fully God and fully human, experienced every human emotion, including falling in love with Mary Magdelene and expressing that love sexually. But like most of Jesus' human aspects, this part of his story was omitted from the Bible.

I: Because it would make him too human. Your disciples, your people who were around then, needed a spiritual leader who was not quite human, who did not have all of the "negative" aspects of being human. In that time period, sexuality was a negative aspect. And so things were covered over.

J: They wanted to protect his image so they just left certain things out.

I: Your Christ figure chose to believe in the principal that all are created equal also. Have you heard much about your women in this time period?

J: At that time women were very subservient.

I: And, in the last 200 years after his death, there were many women who were in the churches in the lead of this spiritualness, this spiritual advancement, and you have not heard of them, either.

J: That's true. All you hear about are the male popes.

I: You do, indeed, but then again, it has been males who have written and rewritten your Bible from the time that it began.

J: So they intentionally left females out.

I: Indeed, they did. And before that, in your Old Testament, they did not leave females out, but they put their entire weight upon them.

Again, it was written by males, and males at that time period were into controlling those whom they thought of as the weaker sex.

There is a great deal of jealousy in the human male personality. Women, from the time they have begun, have been responsible for creating what has been a cross for most human males to bear.

At that time, it was something they could not do. And so it was something that they were very angry about and they began to try to control females. You see, it did really matter who was strongest in those time periods. Let us say, physical strength. And so, who was strongest ruled.

And so this is how it began. But your Jesus Christ figure was much more equal in his thinking and chose to have many friends around him who were female. And this was not something that was a happy thought for most males. It was, indeed, something frowned on. There are many parts of your Bible that are not there.

J: What happened to them?

I: You have people in power. You have people who have translated the Bible so many times, and if they found something that was not conducive to their thinking, they would let it go.

J: Like the part about reincarnation?

I: Yes. It has been changed through many, many years of translation by whoever was in control at the time.

J: Were there any parts that somebody has hidden which will someday emerge and be put back in?

I: Some of them have already emerged and will be translated eventually. Your Dead Sea scrolls have a great amount of information that has not been translated as of yet, and indeed most of your churches would not want it to be translated.

J: Why is that?

I: Because it has parts in it that are not accepted at this time.

J: Like what?

I: It is, for example, dealing with women, reincarnation, and with other principles of behavior. And so it is not something that most of your priests wish to have known. Again there is a tendency for a desire for controlling these things that is happening even now. And so many of these articles are being controlled by a few people who do not wish this knowledge to come out. Even to read these things, it is also a great deal of control, power. There are many things on your earth plane at this time that those who are in power and control will not share with you. But eventually all will come out.

Jesus had the power to transmute his energy into more than just one body during his lifetime and could be in several places at once. Through his focused energy, he could create objects out of nothing. One legend has him in India where he manifested a rose out of thin air. Isabelle verified that he and others could do so, but only if it is not for greed.

I: You have some very advanced human beings who choose to do that as a way of showing people that you can have abundance as well as manifestations of the positive. But you also have several souls who can do this by sheer use of energy from themselves. They can manifest gold and many other things. You have many of these beings in your Tibetan areas, Indian, from India, those places where those souls do nothing but choose to manifest different things as a way, again, of visual lessons. But it is not for greed. And those scientists, alchemists, who try to do this out of metals, base metals, are doing so for power, control, and greed, and it did not come about in that way.

J: How did Jesus learn to do miracles?

I: Well, first we'd like to tell you something about myths. Let's say you were a wonderful football player in your high school and made a touchdown which saved the game for everyone. That touchdown will become much greater in your life as the years go by. The memories will be beautiful and exciting, and you will think back to that time of extreme confidence, happiness, and beauty in that memory.

And this is what is happening to your philosophies regarding any number of your sacred objects. Your Jesus was given the opportunity to use the powers which almost everyone of you can use. Just as those of you who are psychic, healers, or teachers, those of you who have any number of talents...where did you learn them, my friend? You did not. They were within you, were they not?

J: That's right. We were born with them.

I: This is the same as your Jesus. The talents were within when he came. It does not mean that he was an extraordinary power, an extraordinary half-man, half-God. You're all half-man, half-God. But your Jesus was given the knowledge that he had those powers intact into the self.

And he performed miracles without thinking. It was not a philosophy of his. It was not a learning lesson. It was not instruction. It just was a part of himself. And so for him, it was a natural ability.

J: So he really did call forth Lazarus from the dead? And he did all the things that are written about him in the Bible?

I:	Your Lazarus was not, as you know it, dead. But, yes, he did call forth and, yes, that soul came to life once again. But this is the same technique that many of you use to heal parts of the body.

You have some of your people who have these strokes from the head? Have you seen a miracle in that? When someone is completely paralyzed or paralyzed on one side chooses to believe so strongly that he or she will get well? And it happens. Do you consider this abnormal?

J:	No.

I:	Indeed, it is not. And so we tell you that the human mind, the human heart is capable of more than you can ever imagine. Your Jesus did do miracles, but there are many of your souls who do miracles each and every day and do not think about it.

J:	Was Jesus the biological child of Joseph and Mary?

I:	Indeed.

J:	Then why did the Catholic Church launch a huge campaign about the immaculate conception, saying that Mary was a virgin and had not been sexual with Joseph?

I:	The translations of your Bible have gone through many stages. And a great deal of your language, for example, the term virgin, has undergone a metaphorsis. In those times and in those conditions, there was a great desire for productivity on a human level, as in babies. Each and every child who was a female was called a virgin until that personality had a child, and then she was called mother.

But, there is a different reason also for your philosophy of Mary being not touched. It was, again, a way to control women. That you must be pure and chaste in order for a man to take you and have you as a possession. And so, again, there is a great deal of greed and jealousy of women, and men not wanting others to touch or to defile their chosen possessions. And so it came into being that women had to be pure so as not to be soiled goods.

But those two souls took on a commitment of having a child who was extraordinary. And the philosophy of immaculate conception has no bearing in this story.

J: (laughs) It is a story, that's for sure. I was raised Catholic, but I've always found it really hard to believe that a woman would give birth and not have had sexual relations with her husband.

I: There are far stranger things that happened, my friend. You're even doing that now. Your science has produced that very effect at this time.

J: That's true. Test tube babies.

I: Indeed, but it is not so much the story that has power, it is the control.

J: Oh, so the Catholic church used that story to control people.

I: Indeed, not to just control Catholics, but to control women all over of every race.

You see, you have to understand that in that time period, anyone who was thinking of having a wife, had to pay dearly for one. And so they did not want to have another there before them at the gates, if you understand this. There was a great deal of prestige in having children at that time, and they wanted to make sure that they were feeding their own children.

And so women were herded like so many cattle into a small square, and they were not allowed to do much of anything on their own. Women were not allowed to control their own lives because they were a bargaining power for the greatness, enjoyment, and money that a parent could get from that. And, indeed, they were also expected to be chaste and pure so that the other side could feel that he got a good bargain.

And so these stories became much more than they were in the past.

After Jesus was born, Joseph and Mary had other children who, again, were not mentioned in the Bible except for his brother James.

I: If you say to your people, this was a common family— there were brothers and sisters for your Jesus—would that thought make your Jesus more of a man than a Christ? And so this was left out.

J: Now you mentioned Jesus and Mary Magdalene were in love. What did he see in her?

I: He saw beauty, my friend. He saw a personality who was being injured, someone who was being misjudged greatly for her sins and not for the sins of others who used her. Again, it was a double thought process for men, and this was something that your Jesus was trying to change. Again, she had quite a deal of beauty, and she was rather fragile.

Mary Magdalene had been a high priestess who provided a sexual initiation ritual for the young men in the area. As long as she complied with the wishes of those in power, she was accepted in her role. But when she chose to disregard that life and become a follower of Christ, she posed a threat to those in control and so was condemned. Although she and Jesus had three children together, two boys and one girl, they never married.

I: In that time period, a personality who was known as a harlot could not marry. And so, they communed together.

We ask you a question. If you have a group of people who truly believe in the same thing—you call it community or commune—do they not live and eat and breathe and have love and children and the whole thing?

J: Sure.

I: That is somewhat the way it was. Many people traveled with Jesus in groups. Wherever he went, he did not go alone. There were many souls who followed him, and there were large groups of people with him all the time. And this woman was with the group. It was not allowed to marry a woman who was of impurity. It was not allowed by the law of the land.

J: Okay. So they lived outside of the law.

I: You have to understand something. Your Jesus Christ was a rebel. He lived outside of the law of the land most of his life.

J: He sure was a rebel. He came to give a brand new message. So, of course, he was gonna shake up the system that existed then.

I: And what better way to give a brand new message of turning the cheek or of loving your fellow man than to take a woman who was considered impure and not worthy.

J: To show them that she *was* worthy.

I: Each and every soul has a bit of the God in them. And that is what your Jesus was trying to show.

J: That, and practical things like cleanliness is next to godliness. He really recognized that these people didn't take baths and that caused a lot of diseases. So he gave a lot of practical messages for us as well.

I: Yes. Do you think that a god would only give divine messages or would the god give something for those mere human beings to think about and incorporate into their own lives and make them better?

But a great many people in control would have you believe that your God or your Jesus Christ or whatever you choose to call a savior or a messiah, would only give divine messages.

The Biblical account of Easter week, including Jesus' ordeal carrying the cross, has accurately portrayed Jesus' courage and our inhumanity to man.

I: There is not one of you who are considered Christian who could not fail to feel humbled or feel sorrow at a personality crawling through the streets, being tortured, and having to carry his own death implement.

And so, that was great drama and it made those who were in the faith, this new philosophy, become enraged with those who were in power. Again, it was a way of allowing those souls who wished to ferment opinion against those in power to have the backing of the common man.

And so, that, my friend, is very true. That was a tortuous session and, yes, it did happen.

J: When Jesus was laid in the tomb, was he really dead or was it just an out of the body thing? I mean, he did come back, he did resurrect into a transformed being, right?

I: Indeed, he did. But when he was laid in the tomb, he had not passed over yet. You call this condition a coma, and this is what it was.

J: But when he reappeared to Mary Magdalene and the others, why didn't they recognize him when he first came out of the tomb?

I: Because he had gone through a period of cleansing. He had gone through a period of healing, and he was different looking. Have you ever looked upon yourself when you have been very ill, indeed? And then a short time later, have you looked upon yourself once again. Do you feel that you look the same?

J: Not at all.

I: It's amazing what things can be done with a bit of water and clean cloth. But he did arise. He did pass over at that time, but it was not as one thinks.

Your Jesus had an ability to leave the body and stay in the etherical body. And when he chose to let go of the human body, he left. We think that you call this "ascension." The same as your people from Atlantis who had the same ability, by the way. Death was not something to be feared. When those souls wished to leave, they just walked away from the body.

And your Jesus Christ felt that the work was done where he was, and so he chose to walk away from the body.

Again, in this time period, a new philosophy was beginning, a new era was arriving, and those who wished to have that philosophy become stronger than any other philosophy needed to make legends out of the things that your Jesus has done.

He had a great many powers. He had a great many talents, indeed, but if we were to say to you that your Jesus was let down off the cross because he was thought to be dead, but in reality was in a coma, would that have made you feel much better?

You see, they were hoping that souls did not feel better. They were hoping that there would be outrage, that there would be a turning away from the other philosophies, and so it had to be as critical as possible. It had to be as horrible and as mystical as possible.

Now if we were to say to the common, average human being that when someone feels as if his or her work is done, he or she chooses to walk away from his or her body, how many of your souls would find that rather ridiculous?

J: Most of them.

I: Indeed, because most of you have a great deal of fear about your death. And so there is a tendency for those souls who were keeping the faith, who were guarding the philosophies, to have to have something that would make people wonder.

The transfiguration, when Jesus was given a body of light and ascended into heaven, was a visual way of teaching us the need for change. His followers needed to have a vision of the transfiguration in order to spread the word about it. Miriam likened the transfiguration to traveling on the astral plane. When Jesus got through traveling, he came back into his physical body and lived to an old age!

J: His physical body didn't die until he was 77?

M: Indeed, it did not. Why do you think that there are stories all over your world of a person like your Jesus? In every single culture, you will find a personality that is a Jesus.

J: Well, they have a coin of him in India with his face on it. And they have scrolls of things he said in Tibet, so he was in Tibet.

M: Your Native Americans also have stories of him. And so do some of your cultures in Ghana and some in Brazil and some all over your earth.

J: So when he left his physical body for good, what happened to it? Wasn't Jesus an Essene, and didn't he give his body over to Joseph of Arimathea for keeping? Is that what Joseph of Arimathea took to England?

M: Yes. It was buried in a catacomb-like cavern.

J: Will we ever discover that?

M: No, you shall not. Because if you do, that will be the end of your Christianity. Again, you need a deity. You need someone who is so unearth-like that you can honor him as you do your Creator. Does this bother you?

J: No, I think it's fascinating. And the body that we saw go up in the ascension was just his light body?

M: Yes. We were just going to say that to you. You are beginning to read our minds!'

J: (laughs) I know! Isn't that fun?

M: When the personality known as Jesus resurrected, that body transferred to other places. And then the etheric body came back into the physical body.

J: And then at that point, what happened?

M: Then he began to teach more souls.

J: How come that isn't written about?

M: Why should it be? You see, your people were very simple in their thinking. Would it be interesting for you to say to your early Christians that your Jesus is now teaching someone in the Americas? It would be abandonment, would it not? And they needed a martyr.

J: That's true. It wouldn't have been a good story. They had to change the ending a different way.

M: But you see, those souls didn't even know that. It's as if you choose not to see what you see. Let us say to you that those souls who saw the ascension chose not to think about the human body.

J: So he lived on into his 70's.

M: Indeed. And that was his own choosing, to leave. He grew very tired of the earth plane. It was very dense, for the light that he was. And so when he had done his work, he chose to come back to our side. And again he did so as such, he left the body.

J: Just left it behind like discarding a coat.

M: Or a walnut.

J: (laughs) Okay. Now back to Joseph of Arimathea when he went to England. It is said that the Holy Grail was put in the Glastonbury Abbey there.

M: Indeed.

J: Is that the real chalice that was used in the Last Supper?

M: No, it is not.

J: What happened to the real one?

M: It was handed from soul to soul who continued the work.

J: And where is it now?

M: Israel. Near the birthplace.

J: Did Jesus ever go back to see his children or Mary Magdalene?

M: Yes. He lived long enough to see his children grow up.

J: Oh, that's neat. I'm so curious about Jesus because the more I know about him, the more I love him even more. Because he *was* human.

M: You know what would really be interesting, my friend, is if you could love the vibration of your Jesus without knowing anything.

Not many of us realize what a superb psychologist Jesus was, but Isabelle explained how his miracles worked to get our attention.

I: Is it not wonderful that your Jesus Christ figure did so many miracles? Again, he needed to show through visions because human beings choose not to believe in the positive. If he were to come to you and say, "I am a teacher, my friend, and I will teach you these simple rules, how to live your life in a joyful way. I will teach you that it is much better to love one another. I will teach you that it is much better to turn away from anger. I will teach you that it is much better to share." Do you think many human beings would find that a wonderful human being to talk to or to deal with? They would not have the time, my friend. They would need to have visions to make it all wonderful and glorious.

You see, there are many of you who are Jesus Christs right now in this incarnation. But how many of you are listened to? When you try to teach your world, my friend, that human beings should honor their children, how many listen? When you try to teach your world that positivity is a grand way to go, how many listen?

You are all of the same material as your Jesus Christ. You're all brothers under the skin and sisters. But how many are listened to? And unless there is some sort of vision, some sort of difference that others consider interesting or abnormal or exciting, there is not a great deal of listening.

J: Did Jesus always know he was the Christ or did he come into that knowing gradually?

I: Let us ask you. Do you know you are part of the God?

J: Yes.

I: And when did you learn this?

J: Well, I was told this when I went to Catholic grammar school.

I: And we ask you when you learned this? With your heart.

J: I'm not sure of the date or day.

I: We say to you that when your Christ came into being, he did not know that he was special, either. It grew upon him as those who lived with him and loved him told him.

The stories of his birth, the stories of his childhood, it was something that was given to him, and then he became knowledgeable through meditation, through higher looking, the higher self. But we say to you that each and every one of you are Christ. But how many believe it?

J: That's true. Christians claim to be, but they don't really act like it.

I: They do not believe it, also. If there is any soul who comes into your world who says, "I am the Christ," or "I am a Christ," they will soon put him away in a little building where he cannot get out. And so the purpose of a great many of his miracles, of the visions that others saw from him, were a way to get their attention.

Human beings get bored awfully easy, my friend, and they needed something to become enthralled with. Otherwise, there would not have been miracles performed.

J: How did Jesus learn the techniques that he used?

I: Your Jesus studied with many, many souls. He wasn't just in what you now call Jerusalem. But a lot of his wisdom came through meditation. It was not so much the human beings that he dealt with so much.

There was a greater purpose. Besides, this soul as he grew did not have the veil of forgetfulness. So he was in communication with his God.

Again, we tell you that most of you could do the same thing. Has it not been interesting that, when you choose to believe in yourself, you can create miracles and do things that you never thought you could do?

J: Yes, because there's no doubt.

I: Indeed, and that is as it was with that soul.

But your Jesus Christ was not as special as you think he was. He was a spark off the Creator just as you are. But what he did with his spark was something different than most human beings deal with.

He was also of the angelic force. He came into humanness to experience humanness and to help the human being, but he was also a part of that force that you call angelic.

J: Good. I have another question about Christ. You said that he was back in the blend. What did you mean by that?

I: Meaning that that entity chose to reconnect with the force you call Creator.

J: But there are people here who claim to be channeling Sunanda, who is supposed to have been Christ.

I: Let us ask you a question. If you once have a shadow, do you ever get rid of that shadow? The soul has many shadows, and once a soul has been in life or in form of any kind, including angelic, there are shadows left over. In each and every personality, there are memories; there is the whole lifetime in evidence. And when you come to us and take that coat off of that personality, you still have a coat. You still have those memories, those words. The essence of that personality is still in the warehouse.

Even though the soul may choose to pass into the blend, the essences of all personalities are still at reach.

Let's say to you again, if you think of yourself as a whole, then most of the whole is a soul, is it not? And those parts of yourself that you call personalities are shadows. What makes you think that just because your soul goes on into a new personality, it does not mean that you have no chance to speak and communicate with the former personality? Just because you have traded one shadow for another does not mean that that shadow evaporates.

It is an accumulation of all that you have learned as that personality. It is an accumulation of all that you have done in that personality form and all that is for that personality.

It does not mean that that personality you have dies. The soul incorporates a new shadow, a new personality and the old personality, let's say your father, for instance, may choose to take off the coat of your father's personality, and the soul may choose to go on after that into another life, onto higher learning, into another dimension. But the personality that was your father still has the essence of life.

J: Does that last forever?

I: Indeed it does.

J: So John Mark Hammer, who claims to be channeling Jesus (Jeshua), is telling the truth?

I: He's reaching the personality of the soul. Just because the soul chooses to go on and incorporate into the blend does not mean that there are not essences of personalities still within the warehouse.

J: Now will the soul that has been incorporated into the blend ever come out again?

I: Yes. Does not your God come out again? Is it not part of the whole? You see there are many people who think that those who go into the blend or go into the whole, tend to disappear. But why would you think they would disappear? The whole is all around you. It is all part of you.

And so it is not that they are hiding somewhere, that they have disappeared. It is that they have incorporated into a great, bigger picture.

And so many of you think that when you regroup with the God, then you disappear; your soul disappears. But, in reality you become much more than you ever have been. It's as if you have a great deal of immense power behind you.

And so, yes, in reality many of the souls on your plane can get in touch with the essences of Abraham Lincoln, Jesus Christ, Mohammed, Confuscius, any of those souls that you choose to get in touch with. It is not necessarily the soul that you are touching. But you can all contact the shadow of that soul who committed to be your Jesus Christ.

And it is interesting that you say he was the son of God with such reverence because you all are the sons of God and the daughters of God. And so it becomes not such a reverent thing, does it not? It is just that this soul came as a teacher, and the teaching that he gave was to love one another as you would yourself.

But that even has become misconstrued in some humans' minds and in some ways in your Bible. Your Bible is an interesting book. It is a work of art. But you can find each and every side of any argument, any thought process in your Bible. It is something that is equal on all sides and, except for the parts that have been stolen, it is a work of art and a good book to read and follow a great many of the aspects of the wording.

Many people will spout a Biblical quotation to finish off an argument, but when one looks hard enough, one will find the exact opposite point of view in the Bible. Isabelle maintained that people who use the Bible like that are trying to gain control.

I: That is one of the major lessons that most of you need to learn as of yet, to let go of control of others especially. It is one of the last lessons that you will have to learn. It is the hardest lesson to let go of.

J: Controlling others?

I: Indeed, because if you let go of control, are you someone in your mind? And if you are not someone, then why are you here? You understand? If you cannot prove that you are special, then you have no choice but to leave. In some people's minds, this is so.

Jesus' Mother, Mary

Like Jesus, his mother, Mary was part of the angelic force who came in to enlighten people and give them something to hope for. Unlike Jesus, she has opted not to come back to earth again except in apparitions as a way of uplifting humanity.

J: There are many sightings of Mary around the world, at Fatima and different places.

I: She has chosen not to come back again. But again, she chooses to do her work in this form as a way of, again, miracles. Human beings need these visions to believe in themselves and in the goodness of humanity.

And so she has chosen to do her work in that way. She has not blended with the Creator as of this time because she can use her name to create more learning and more progress.

J: Does she have any particular message that she'd like to give us at this time?

I: She says for you to love the children, that they are the hope of your future, and to allow them to become more than they can be.

It is an interesting thing that most human beings do not allow their children to see, to remember, to deal with their high spiritual selves. It is something that is frowned upon because there is much fear. When children begin to discuss things that they have no knowledge of, there is a tendency to have a great deal of fear.

And so it would be wonderful to allow children to be the miracles they are. But we have been saying that for eons of time. We do hope someone is listening.

J: I hope so, too, because children need to be honored and not ignored.

I: And so do all human beings.

Assassinations

Hollywood movies and popular novels have speculated about the death of president John F. Kennedy. The lone gunman theory, the findings of the Warren commission, and allegations of a government conspiracy—all have intrigued the

American public for years. Isabelle offered the angel's account of this profound tragedy, as well as the unfortunate deaths of Bobby Kennedy and Dr. Martin Luther King, Jr. First, the Kennedy assassination.

Besides Harvey Oswald, there was another man on the ground who shot the president. This man went undetected because most people were pointing and looking at Oswald perched in a building window. Several high government officials are aware of this second man, who was killed to silence his involvement. Not only was President Lyndon Johnson involved in the assassination, but so were the CIA and the Mafia.

I: Your President Kennedy stepped on a lot of toes. There were a lot of people in your higher government who felt that he was not a good example for Americans at that time.

J: Why is that?

I: There was a great fear that many of his faults would become known. And at that time, human beings had a very black and white attitude of those in government. Again, he was a personality who was very head-strong and chose not to allow others to lead him or to help with the ruling of the government.

And for those who desired a great deal of power, there needed to be an ending to that. Your President Johnson knew about this and was one of the people who absolutely hated the control of the man you call Kennedy.

He was belittled a great deal by Kennedy, and there was a tendency for him to want to get even. He was also a personality who craved power above all.

J: Yeah. I could tell from the smirk on his face as he was being sworn in. It was like he was pretending to be sad, but he wasn't.

I: He was enlightened at that moment.

J: What about President Kennedy's brother, Bobby Kennedy? Was there a conspiracy involved with that?

I: Indeed.

J: Who else besides Sirhan Sirhan?

I: Again, your Mafia.

J: Oh. And does anybody know about that connection in the government?

I: Yes.

J: Will that ever come out to the American public?

I: No.

J: What about Martin Luther King?

I: It was a conspiracy with your FBI and J. Edgar Hoover. And the interesting thing about this is that they procurred people who had a great hatred for your black personalities and used that as a way of killing this man. He was getting too powerful.

J: Right. But the FBI helped in that?

I: Indeed. You see, there is much that your Americans do not understand about their government. Those who ruled, especially from the '40s to the '70s, had a tendency to be power hungry and power crazy. They viewed power with greed.

So they did things that were unthinkable and that your American people could not believe, just as in your Viet Nam war. Again, this was a greedy thing to do. People wanted power and money, and so there was a tendency to need a war, and your American public, for the most part, could not believe that their government could do such a thing.

J: Right. Well, that's why they protested so much. They didn't believe in that war.

I: Indeed. But how many of them did because the government told them to.

J: That's true. They made up a reason and everybody bought it because that's what they wanted to believe, I guess. And they had people like Jane Fonda trying to say there's another way of looking at it, and they all hated her for awhile.

I: Indeed they did, but you must understand that this young woman did things in a very negative way and did things in order to enrage the American public.

J: Yes. Well, she succeeded in doing that.

I: She surely did and had to pay for it. If she had done things in a different way, my friend, she would not have had the problems that she had. There are many things that your government has fingers in, even your UFO activity has a great deal to do with power and greed. Your government is very aware of what has been happening with many sightings.

J: Will they ever be honest with us about anything?

I: If they can help it, they will not.

J: Because knowledge is power, right?

I: Indeed. It is a heady feeling, is it not, to know something that others do not know.

J: Well, that's true. Except it's so selfish and self-serving.

I: Do you think that this is not a part of those who are in power? In fact, your world will never become right or positive until you get rid of the need for greed and power.

J: That means the total restructuring of our government, then, because the way it's set up now gives them total power.

I: Indeed, it will be so, eventually. But it takes a beginning. Each and every human being needs to begin to let go of that need for power and greed, that need to have all the material things about him, that need to say, "This is mine and you cannot have it," that need to say, "Look what I have and you do not."

And eventually if every human being does this, you will not have the need to have those people in power.

Marilyn Monroe

The untimely death of Marilyn Monroe has never really been explained away, leaving us questioning why, despite insecurities and neuroses, a beautiful actress would end her life at the height of her career. David shed some light on what happened to this famous actress.

D: She was a person who was in the middle of something that was bigger than she was. There was a tendency for her to be very thoughtless in her talk and in her thinking and she was put to death.

J: By whom?

D: Again, in collusion with your government, and the CIA, was your Mafia. *In fact, we tell you a secret.* There are many of your deaths which are contracted out by your government to this organization.

J: Did the government pay the Mafia to do her in?

D: Indeed, they did because she was upsetting your apple cart. This was a young woman who chose to be thoughtless in her speech. She spoke out and threatened and chose to do things that were not pertinent to her welfare. And so she was silenced.

J: Did John Kennedy or his brother Robert have anything to do with that?

D: No. There were certain powers behind those two people who looked out for their well being. And the time period that you are speaking of, there was not allowed a breath of scandal. And so they were looked after.

M: She was also being used as punishment for Bobby Kennedy because he had become too hot on the trail of some of the Mafia godfathers. This was a warning. If they could get to his paramour, then they would get to his family next.

D: She did overdose on drugs, but it was not of her taking. There are always those behind the power who will see to it that nothing comes of anything to do with scandal, if it will interfere with those people in power.

Miriam interjected that the Mafia had forced Marilyn to swallow drugs, but what really killed her was a shot of nembutol which they adminstered rectally. The L.A. coroner was told to be very careful how he printed his report because the CIA would make him and his family pay for any slip-up.

J: Are the people who are responsible for her death still alive?

D: Indeed.

J: Will it ever come to light who was responsible?

D: Not if they can help it. But do you think that this is new and interesting? It is not. It has always been so.

Actually the chaos in your earth at this time is rather refreshing because truth is coming out more and more each day and many of you are scandalized and threatened by such truths from all around your world, but this is indeed good because you no longer hide that which you fear.

And so there is room for improvement. There is room for growth when you have truths coming out.

J: Yes, we've been in denial too long.

D: A great deal of the time, let us say, since your world began.

J: (laughs) That's a long time.

D: And one word will tell you why you all do this so much. It is called judgment.

J: So when we can stop judgment, then our reality shifts.

D: Indeed, it does.

Richard Nixon

Although there have been many words written on the resignation of president Richard Nixon, we couldn't help but ask Safar what drove Nixon to his involvement in Watergate and what was on the 18 minutes of erased tape.

S: Power. This was a human being who felt the need for power greatly. He needed to show his loved ones that he could be someone powerful and felt very powerless. And the 18 minutes of tape dealt with his incrimination of self. It dealt with his need for power and with his demand for those to do what needed to be done. And when he left your power place...

J: The White House.

S: ...he indeed felt put upon and rejected. He indeed did not truly understand why those of you who rejected him could not again love him. This is a personality who chose the quick way to power and paid the price very heavily indeed. But we do say to you that he came along, and he chose to change. And he became more powerful than he could have ever been.

J: Yes, writing his books and doing work with foreign countries

S: Indeed.

J: What was his relationship with his wife, Pat, like after Watergate?

S: There was a great deal of anger and angst with him towards the wife, and she became the scapegoat and went into drink to escape his anger. But as he grew older, and as he began to realize what true power was, there was a great love for each.

J: How's he doing now?

S: He is very serene and very happy with what he accomplished towards the end of his life. He realizes now that power is not a substance to grab at, but is a way of dealing with humanity.

Jacqueline Kennedy Onassis

America truly grieved at the passing of Jackie Kennedy Onassis. Although she never believed the Warren Commission findings on her husband's death, she attributed his assassination to the act of a mad man. She felt this was the safest approach to take because she had two little children to protect, and if she had begun to believe all that she'd heard, she would have gone literally insane.

The lowest point of her life was when, out of loneliness, she married Aristotle Onassis.

J: He left her pretty much emotionally unattached and went off with Maria Callas, his old girlfriend.

M: But, that is something that she did not expect.

J: Did she hold it against him?

M: No, she held it against herself and her self-esteem grew very low at that time. It was the lowest part of her life.

J: What was the happiest part? With her grandchildren?

M: This last ten years with the man.

J: Oh, Maurice Tempelsman.

M: Yes. Her grandchildren gave her great pleasure, but you see your lady Jackie has always been a solitary human being. She had great pride in her children, but she also allowed them to become independent and to let go of them. And in the very end of her life, she derived great pleasure from Maurice.

J: But he was already married so she could not marry him.

M: And that, indeed, was safe, for Jackie had begun to believe that anyone she married would be under a curse. She had the feeling in this lifetime that most of everything would be taken away from her. It was always so from the time she was a small child. And so this one thing could not be taken away because it wasn't hers in the first place.

And with her children, there was also a great desire to protect them and leave them with a fortune so that they could do what they had to do.

J: Are either one of them going into politics?

M: Indeed, they will. Caroline.

J: What about John?

M: John is much more interested in your drama.

J: Yes, he's been doing some television hosting.

M: Eventually he will try to go into a bit of politics as a way of remembering and honoring his parents, but it is not what he really wishes to do.

J: How's she doing on the other side?

M: She is resting. There has been a joyful reunion. It is interesting that she had a horse that she loved a great deal, and even that horse came to the reunion.

J: What was the horse's name, do you know?

M: We have no inkling of it, but it was a small horse, a pony.

J: Did John Kennedy come to the reunion?

M: Yes.

J: Was she surprised to see him?

M: No. She was waiting for him to take her home. You see, the interesting thing about that relationship is they were friends more than they were married partners. She knew about the affairs and chose to overlook them for protection of her children.

J: She knew about Marilyn Monroe?

M: Indeed. And chose to overlook that also because in her mind it was her duty. When you are serving the nation, you must serve them to the fullest of your ability.

J: So she thought it was more responsible on her part to ignore his weaknesses and protect her children. And I think she thought her role was really as a mother first.

M: Indeed it was. She was never comfortable with what you
call celebrity status.

Chapter 8

Current Lessons

To forgive is divine. One of your people said that.
That is so. But to see the lessons in that forgiveness
or in that cruelty is even more important.

Love of Self

T hose of us on our spiritual path use rituals, crystals, prayer mats, incense, whatever it takes for us to believe our connection to God is solid. But as Isabelle so wisely pointed out, the bottom line is self-esteem, which we need in order to accept what we so ardently pray for.

I: Everything in your earth is accomplished through your own power, my friend. There is something important to say about your own powers. If you do not feel that you have your own power, we guarantee you that you will not, and no one can give you the power if you will not accept it.

So, look into the whole and not just a part of yourselves. Many of you use rituals in order to slide through life. If we use a small ritual as, let us say, the Lord's Prayer, then that will take care of everything. And they fail to realize that it is a lot more work than that.

There must be a looking and a cleansing of the humanness. Then and only then can you develop your power. All things that happen to you, be they positive or negative, are through your own power. Your God does not do things, either positively or negatively, to you and neither does your devil. It is your personality—your very self—who will give and take from yourself. We do not say to you that angels and your God cannot give your miracles. But you must use the whole to ask.

J: Yes. I've studied Hawaiian metaphysics called Huna. "Huna" in Hawaiian means "the secret," and what they teach is that the secret to getting a prayer answered is for your subconscious mind, your "little self," to feel worthy, to feel guilt-free. It can look up in the face of the big God, the "big self," and ask for a prayer. It's when it doesn't feel worthy, when it feels like it has sinned or it feels like it's not deserving, that the prayer doesn't get through because the little self won't turn its face up and ask for what it wants.

I: Indeed. *We say to you a little secret.* To believe is not the same thing as to know. And if you wish to have those things which you consider positive come to you, you must *know*. You must know that it is part of your personality, part of your power, to accomplish these things. Now, there is direct intervention at times of your God, of your angels and guides, but most of the time, you must learn how to use your power. There have been times far past where human beings knew more about their power than almost anything else and then fear set in.

J: What caused it all to start? What caused the big fear?

I: You became too powerful and too greedy, and then there was fear of those who were powerful and greedy. There was fear that you may not have been as powerful as the other.

And so your power went away, and now human beings, except for a few, are almost powerless. They are like little leaves fluttering in the wind. They have no idea that they can control their own lives.

J: Yes, so that's what we need to learn, that we have the power within to change our world.

I: Indeed, you do. And there is a force, a benevolent force, that will intercede at different times in your life. You have all felt this at some point. But, for the most part, it is because you truly desired an intercession, and you truly believed it was, for yourself, a good thing.

Now there are many of your folk who choose to constantly ask for riches, and your God, even though you're not aware of this, realizes that it is not a good thing for you, and so do your guides.

J: So you don't get it.

I: Indeed. Most human beings tend to think that riches, your money, will make everything all right and that, indeed, is not so. It is a good thing for many of you to have these riches. It makes a balance. It also helps you to strive for whatever you can be. But most of you feel deep in your hearts that if you had money, then you would not have the problems that you have now. That is not so. And in fact, for most of you who are in turmoil, you would have more problems. And indeed it would bring much fear into your life.

J: Well, they say "the love of money is the root of all evil," that attachment to money.

I: And we say to you, humanness is the root of all evil.

J: Really?

I: Indeed, it is, for you make it up yourself. And that, my friends, is the last remaining amount of power that you truly have. The rest is rusty. It does not mean that you have lost your power. It means that you have not used it and you need to practice.

But the one power that you have retained in your human forms is negativity. And so, that is quite an easy thing to do, is it not?

How many of you feel that if you thought of something that was a very negative thought, all of a sudden it happened to you, was that not a frightening thing? It was a coincidence? No, it was not. You brought that upon yourselves by your fear and by adding that power to your fear.

J: So, when we work on reclaiming our sense of power, what's the first thing we need to be aware of?

I: Love of self. It's the hardest lesson you'll have to learn, but, indeed, that is what will give you your power for the positivity back.

J: Is there something we can say to ourselves every day to increase our love for ourselves?

I: You can look in your mirror and you can say, "I believe in myself."

That's what you have to do as a start. "I allow myself to believe in myself. I allow myself to be beautiful. I allow myself to be positive. I allow myself to be in abundance and I deserve." Any number of these things will help, indeed. But until you cleanse that heart of yours of all that pain and all those feelings of inferiority, you are not going to do very much at all because you will truly not believe.

J: We have to reconnect the heart to the mind.

I: Indeed. We ask you if you were to throw a beautiful diamond into a cesspool, would you be able to find it?

J: (laughs) It'd be kind of hard.

I: Indeed. And that is what your hearts are at this time. Your very self is a cesspool, and all that negativity that you have had for so long about yourself and from yourself and even from others is a cesspool. And when you begin to work on positivity, when you begin to work on love of self, it is like throwing a beautiful diamond into the cesspool and you spend many, many hours trying to find it and cannot.

AIDS

Behind every trauma suffered by humanity is a lesson that needs to be learned. Even when we're facing worldwide devastation with impending epidemics, such as with AIDS, there are heavy lessons presented to us.

I: It is a two-fold lesson, my friend. The first part of that lesson is to show your world how very sick it is, the people of the world, the thinking of the world, the greed of the world, the me of the world. But that is a minor purpose.

The major purpose of the disease AIDS is a lesson in compassion. It is the greatest lesson in compassion that humanity will ever learn. There will be almost two-thirds of your world's population affected with this disease at some time or other.

It is also a way of cleansing the population, but you have to understand, this is not another big purpose. The main reason for the AIDS epidemic is a lesson in compassion. We tried this during your World War II. We tried this during your eras of the 30s. We tried this during your Black Plagues, your plagues of leprosy, many other times, but it has not been able to be fulfilled as lessons. If you can reach out through your very fears of death to touch the hand of another who has this disease, to put your arms around another who has this disease and fears his or her own death, then you will have learned the greatest act of compassion that a human being can learn. And until you learn this lesson, you cannot fully go on. And if it is not the AIDS epidemic, it will be something else. This is just a catalyst for that lesson. The virus, as you know it, will never have a cure. But you can understand that at one point your scientists will find a vaccination.

J: To prevent it?

I: Indeed. But, it will not be until there has been great damage to the human race.

J: Two-thirds of the population sounds like a great bit of damage.

I: We say almost two-thirds. But, indeed, it will not be very much less. Even now, many of your little souls, your babies that are being born, have this disease. And many more human beings have this disease without realizing it. It can take up to twenty years of your life to have this disease and not know of it. And then there is a trigger point, and you become aware of it. But again we tell you it is one of the greatest lessons that has been put into force in your world of compassion, and human beings cannot become that which they choose to become without compassion.

J: So once they learn that lesson, there's no need for AIDS.

I: And we do not say to you that you have to cleanse the person's body, that you have to feed the person, that you have to give the person injections. We say to you to reach out through your fears, and the very strongest fear in humanness is death. And that is why it's very frightening. And that is why it is the greatest lesson of compassion. If you put your arms around another and you say to that person, "Let me hold you. Let me feel the love for you," you will have learned this lesson. And until many people do this, you will not have even a vaccination.

J: Could you tell us when the vaccine would be developed?

I: It is already in the planning stages.

J: Is it being developed here in our country?

I: No, it is not.

J: Which countries will be most likely to be affected by the AIDS epidemic?

I: Africa, America, Russia, Sweden, and Japan. Some of your countries will keep silent about their "shame."

J: Like maybe China?

I: Indeed. In fact, those people found to have that virus will be put to death as a way of combating this disease.

J: Yes. I thought that today as I was writing this question. And that is exactly what came to mind.

I: That is because you felt truth.

J: Now, if diseases like AIDS or cancer are in our system already, how come they don't bloom fully in all people? The AIDS virus does not come out in about 10% of the population that have HIV positive signs in them. The same thing with cancer. We have cancer roaming around our bodies and yet some people will develop the disease and some won't. Why is that?

I: When you have things roaming around in the body, you have movement, do you not? But, you have to have a catalyst to make that movement mutate. And most of you who have cancer or AIDS mutating into the body as a very strong disease do so by the use of—your terms—stress, anger. All the negative aspects of the human body and mind contribute to mutation. And some of you choose not to be bothered by things within the body you cannot see or deal with on a logical level. There is a great deal to say about letting go of anger and stress in good ways.

J: Yeah. I know when I started thinking of people I really had a problem with in my past, you know, just the image of them makes me angry. But now I realize that we all played a part in a drama, and that I should really thank them for the lessons that they brought me rather than to hold grudges or be angry. I'm trying to see it from a different perspective.

I: Indeed. But that's because of your growth. You must understand something. They are part of the scenario. They came to help you build a play so that you can learn the lessons. If you did not have the scenario that these people contributed to, you would not be able to learn the lessons.

Let us take abuse. If you do not have abuse as a child, then you cannot learn what abuse feels like. You cannot learn to overcome the feelings of anger, to forgive, or to have courage. You cannot learn to stand up for self, to begin to love self. And you cannot learn to speak out to others on that aspect of yourself. At some point, everyone who has had abuse in his or her lifetime will speak out or act out. And some choose to act out negatively, and some choose to act out positively, but it is still balance.

So you must thank those souls who indeed were very cruel to you or unkind or absent-minded or stupid, because they contributed to the scenario so that you might learn those very important lessons and balance them.

J: Right. In looking back on it, I can see that. When I was in the middle of it, though, it was hard to see.

I: Indeed. But it is hard to see behind you, is it not?

J: (laughs) Yeah.

I: All right. We say to you that that is growth, my friend. When you can begin to see all sides of the question or picture, then you have truly grown. We do not say that it is bad or good to see a picture or not to see a picture. We say to you that this is learning the lesson. To forgive is divine. One of your people said that. That is so. But to see the lessons in that forgiveness or in that cruelty is even more important.

J: Right. When you see it as a lesson, it makes it easier to forgive the person.

I: Indeed. *And we will tell you a small secret.* Every one of your lessons that are negative, every one of your lessons that are painful, all have but one purpose and that is to teach, be it yourself or another. It is to teach. When you have learned the lesson of abuse, do not most of you who go through the steps of being abused, of saying no, of being angry and of letting go, do not all of you at some point in your life reveal that and help another? That is the purpose, my friend, for everything upon your earth. To teach.

Again, you plan every aspect of your life. Now at one point in your growth, some of you need a little bit of convincing and a little bit of encouragement. And so we try to help you get back when you need to learn certain lessons. And then many of you, when you do come to the earth plane, spend most of your life trying to get out of it. And we are finding that this is not exactly a good thing to do for many of you. And so, we too, my friend, are learning.

Creating Disease

To be human is to have lessons to learn, and the authors are no exception. While Jennifer has suffered from psoriasis for years, Rosie has been asthmatic even longer. But, as David reminds us, behind every physical disease has a spiritual cause.

D: The very fear of not being perfect is why you have psoriasis. You see, you have as near a perfect body as possible, do you not? And the one thing that is an imperfection for you is the skin.

Now when you begin to allow and let go of that need for perfection and that need to be super-human, you will also let go of that skin condition that you desire not to have. It is the one thing in your life that makes you human, my friend.

You see, the interesting part for you souls who are light workers is that you do not truly believe you are human. And in reality you are not, but in your reality, you must appear so.

And with the asthma, this is a case of a personality, who, again, is trying to be everything for everyone and there is a tendency for her to feel miserably at this time. There is also a great need for her to be closeted with herself. And so she allows a disease to come into the mind and body in order to do that.

This one truly does not believe that she deserves rest, as you do not, either. Why do you think you have come together, my friend? You are so very different, are you not? Well, the one thing that brings you together is to work on the feeling of needing to be perfect.

Both of you have a problem with being human. And because you are both light workers, because you both have a very strong purpose for other humanity, there is a great need for you to deal with humanness, and neither of you like it very much.

J: True. (laughs) But we will get through this, won't we?

D: You can achieve and become all that you wish to be within a human mold. And when you come back home with us, there shall be a great reunion, and we shall all have a good laugh over this human thing.

Each and every personality creates a disease, and if it is not just with yourself, it is with your world because you have all helped in creating your world, as in pollution, as in the distribution of emotion; you all have helped to create it in one form or other. There is not a soul on earth who has not helped to create disease.

We do not say this is wrong, but you create your own diseases on a human level, and when you all learn to stop fearing what you most fear, most of your diseases shall go away. When you learn to stop desiring anger as a mode of vocalizing that which you feel, you shall all stop having so many diseases of the body. And so it is a good lesson for everyone to learn, that you must allow yourself to be human. Most of you feel that you come to this earth plane in order to perfect the soul. That is not necessarily true because the soul is already perfected. There is nothing wrong with each and every soul. What you come to do is to perfect the humanness in yourself.

The Environment

One encompassing lesson we are currently learning has to do with the environment. Not only are we contaminating our water supply and food with pesticides, we are damaging our health in insidious ways through electrical power lines which are placed too near our houses.

I: Anyone who partakes of the land that's near these wirings is asking for problems of the body, mind, even the emotions.

J: Well, there have been lawsuits and all the big electrical companies have high-powered lawyers who manage to win these suits. There are children who live near these wires who are being born with cancers which parents know are related to that high voltage, but they can't prove it.

I: They may not be able to. In the future, each and every human being will have to speak up and say his or her piece. And then by popular demand, these things will be taken down and fixed. Even though you put these things under your ground, they still contribute frequencies that cannot be good for the human being to walk upon, but it is a slightly better idea than having them in your air.

Again, we say to you that one or two come forward, three or four, a hundred, but that will not change the tide of greed, my friend, and that's exactly what it is, greed. There are personalities who run your companies who choose not to put these things under ground because it will cost them finances that they could have for their own pockets.

And so, when enough of you souls get together and march and protest that these things are not good, it will change. It is an interesting thing about human beings. If it is not affecting your child, if it is not affecting your life, then it is something that you musn't think about.

J: Yes. We feel disconnected from each other.

I: Indeed, you do. Again as Gabriel has said, the one reason you do not have connection is because the foundations are rotten. So if you clean the foundation of the heart, then the connections will begin.

Again, human beings have a great deal of fear of protecting their own. And so, they do nothing until it is their own that needs the protection. Again, it is greed and a fear of having less than they normally would if they would have to put up a fight.

J: There's a fear of competition.

I: Not only that, your human beings, for the most part, choose to want all these wonderful things to happen to their family, their earth, their planet, but would like somebody else to do the work.

J: (laughs) That's true.

I: Indeed, it is. But until it affects one in your family, then and only then will most human beings become enraged, become self-righteous, and begin to try to change the thinking of those in power. This is where it must end. You must have many, many souls in the future who do not wait until their own kind are hurting.

You must all stand up and say, "We do not wish this to be." And then they will tell you, "Where do you think we shall find the money?" And you all must stick up for this plan by giving a little extra. Humans wish to have many things that are subject to renewal, subject to betterment for the human race, but they do not wish to reach into their pockets.

J: Yes. Gabriel was talking about food being polluted, and it reminded me that some people have made such a big deal about being vegetarians, and they avoid meat because they figure that it's bad for them and eating fruits and vegetables is good. But now, you know, you really wonder, what can we eat that is safe anymore?

I: There is not one thing upon your earth that is safe. Not even the water, my friend. In the name of your science, so many of your products for consumption have been changed.

And that in itself would not have been so very bad, but in the meantime, they are using drastic measures that are very dangerous to your humanness, such as your insecticides. If humans especially in your country do not like what they see, for example, a blemish on a fruit, something that isn't exactly beautiful, the human being will not like to eat it.

Once a great deal of your science was for the good of mankind; it made them a better race of people. But it has gone too far, and this must be taken care of.

J: What about when they radiate food in the grocery stores and it's precisely for the reason that you mentioned, that human beings don't like to have blemishes on their fruit or vegetables. What about that?

I: This procedure will be found to have some dangerous side effects. But again your scientists are trying to find ways to feed more and more of the people of your earth, and so they will go to science more and more. This, in one respect, is a good idea because human beings have over-populated their earth, and there is evidence coming of a very large famine that will cover a great deal of your world. And your scientists know that this shall happen eventually and are trying desperately to make more and more food for humanity. But, in the long run, it will do much damage to the human race.

J: Is that coming very soon?

I: Within seven years. Indeed. It is unimaginable to think that your country at this time could feed a smaller country with just the waste products that you throw away every day.

J: We produce 70% of the world's garbage.

I: Indeed, you do and this, too, shall change. It will get to a point when your scientists will think about taking your garbage out into space. We do hope that most of you try to deny this plan and think of a better solution. There are solutions there.

When your oil becomes less accessible, when you have a fear of your gasoline not being there to take care of your needs, you will be very surprised at some of the answers your scientists will come up with, and using garbage as a way of fuel is one of them.

J: I have a friend who's a professor at a local university, and he invented a process where you can burn old tires and convert them into fuel, but he and others who have had these patents out there have been bought out by the big companies who want to continue selling their expensive gasoline.

I: Isn't that a shame that human beings have such an idea of greed? That one person, for the good of only one, can prevent the good of all others.

The Criminal Element

A sign of our times seems to be an increase in criminal activity resulting in a larger prison population. But the angels maintain that people are coming in to our earth plane to learn both polarities in one lifetime.

I: Many of you need to experience polarities from others on an impersonal level. And so that much more is needed to be done with those souls who commit to be criminals. It is an object lesson. It is an example. And it is the way to change your planet. You need to see balance. You need to see the polarities in order to effect change.

And you humans who have come in so fast at a breakneck speed and who need to learn more, faster, you cannot wait another lifetime. You cannot wait another ten years. And so these souls that you call criminals are coming in with a two-fold purpose: to help those souls begin to assimilate and to think of their philosophies, and to stand out and speak up.

J: If you have a perception that you don't want to be a murderer, is it because you once committed a murder in another lifetime and knew how horrible it was? Are you recalling that horror?

I: Indeed, it is, for the most part. And you know, it is interesting that most of the murders that one recalls are because of war. It has nothing to do with murdering another person on purpose and with cruelty. It is the idea that once you have killed and you see what is left and what has gone on, there is a tendency to feel great remorse. And most of this happens in your wars. Your commanders, your people in power, are making killers of every one of those people in their service. And it is something that everyone will go through and desire not to do again.

Those people who choose to object to your wars, choose to be in philosophies that will not allow killing, they do so, number one, because they came back very fast and, number two, because they have been in many wars, not just one. And they grow sickened at the idea of killing for power.

J: Is there a biology or a science of aggression and violence? In other words, are there chemicals in the body that cause more aggression and violence to come forth?

I: More so there are pollutants that are born within the body that are brought to the child in the womb from the air, from the products that you eat, from the pollutants that the mother ingests, and it is basically more the pollutants that cause some of these changes for aggression.

J: If we clean up the air, if we clean up those pollutants that can affect the fetus in the womb, will we, in turn, start to have fewer violent people in the world?

I: But even those things that you do not think of as pollutants that you put in your food sources are pollutants to some.

Some people have an allergic reaction to your society and to the way you do things and to the chemicals that are put into other animals, into your plant life, into your ground. A very sensitive body can become negative in thinking because of these pollutants.

If you were to try to clean up your entire world, then, yes, something might cause a chain reaction to make children who are not so aggressive. Again, because these pollutants are in the body does not mean the child should not be taught right from wrong.

And there are a great many reasons why human beings become violent and aggressive. Besides pollutants, another reason is that no one chooses to take time very much any more for these little ones who are different. And so, it is as if they are growing alone, and along with the sensitivity, they do not have the training.

J: Right. There's so much child abuse in our country. We have over 5,000 children who die every year because of parental or adult abuse.

I: And a great many of them are affected by stress which is also a pollutant in the system. It is not a chemical, it is not a liquid, but it is a pollutant, and you ingest these stressful things and you become aggressive.

It has always been that the stronger will take out on the weaker those things that it cannot deal with. This is a human way. And many, many souls are involved in chaotic living and thinking and in pollutions of different types, and they choose to take it out on those little souls who cannot fight back.

And so there must be a great deal of change on your earth before the whole can go to a different level.

Justice on Trial

Intense media coverage of recent trials involving the Menendez brothers, Richard Allen Davis and O. J. Simpson has presented us with more lessons to learn about our judicial system. When David was asked if the Menendez brothers would be found guilty, for example, he said it would all depend on whether Californians would loudly voice an opinion on the case.

D: And for every lesson, there is a lesson within the lesson. And your lesson within this lesson is that those folks who choose to abuse children cannot continue to do so. There must be an end to this abuse, and so many of you have a tendency to feel very badly indeed for these young men.

And so that is a lesson within the lesson. On one hand, your judicial system needs to be overturned; on the other hand, you need to have compassion for those who have been hurt so badly. Eventually these souls will be committed and lose everything they have.

J: They've already lost their house, I think.

D: Indeed. There was indeed very strong abuse. It was very bad. But there was also a factor of greed.

J: On their part?

D: Indeed. And this was done with forethought and with malice. Now it will be up to your people to choose which is the most important.

If only the angels could give their account in court of the Polly Klaas tragedy. Richard Allen Davis, the man arrested for the kidnap and murder of Polly Klaas out of her own home, maintained that he killed her because he had been drinking beer and smoking marijuana. But Safar was quick to give a different version.

J: Richard Allen Davis says that she was alive at the time that two sheriff deputies who weren't aware of the kidnapping helped him pull a car from the ditch, and it was because of the drugs in his system that he decided to kill her.

S: That is not so.

J: If she was alive at the time that the deputies were there, why didn't she run?

S: She was not alive.

J: Okay. That's what her grandfather maintains. What was Davis' motive?

S: This fiend takes his joy from fear and from hurting others. And maybe we have not been here (the other side) long enough, and we still have judgment. But we say to you that he is a fiend, and he takes great pleasure in pain of others. He was very much into his head. He understands what he has done, and he does not care.

J: Is it because of drugs?

S: It is not so. He was clear-headed at the time. It is because he has been hurt in his time, and he wishes to do much damage to others so that he can begin to feel again.

This is a person who does not feel, and he wishes to feel. And the only way he has found feeling is to do something so horrible to another human being that it causes a great anguish, a great outcry. And then he begins to feel. And we do say to you he should be tried and justice should be done.

No one will dispute the claim that the O. J. Simpson murder case has been the trial of the century. Near the end of June, 1994, Miriam came through the Isabelle group to tell us the lessons we are to learn from this tragedy as well as the death of Polly Klaas.

M: Once again we will tell you that human beings need to have change in their lives. Human beings tend to learn through violence, through pain, through turmoil, sorrow, negative thinking, and so what is brought about to your world are some lessons that can be very, very traumatic, indeed. We said to you that one being your Polly Klaas? This is another.

Most human beings do not understand violence, but they condone violence by turning their backs and shutting the doors. And so something that is so traumatic needs to be done in order for human beings to open the door wide and to say, "We need change." They need to learn the lesson of change. And yes, there is much violence and, yes, there is much trauma, but nothing ever ends. But those people who have chosen to participate in these lessons are not truly affected forever by it. They are souls that are very old indeed, and they choose to partake in a lesson to teach change to mankind.

Now in the case of Polly Klaas, the trauma was not that a child died, for you see many children die on your earth plane, and we would say 99% of you shake your heads and say, "Tch, tch, tch, tch, tch. That is such a terrible thing." And then you go into your homes and close your doors, and you forget because it is not your family.

The trauma for Polly and for all human beings, we might add, was that this was in her own home where the door had been closed.

J: And she thought she was safe.

M: And so did her parents. And so have many of your souls. Now the man who has killed this child has been apprehended, has he not?

J: Yes, he has.

M: For there it stops for many people, but just the idea of seeing on your televisions the face of a man who can commit such trauma and such evil to be smiling, laughing, and smirking at bereaved parents is enough to make you say, "Enough is enough" of violence.

There are four of these traumas and each one will be dealing with something else. The case of the female and male, the female Simpson is another such lesson. While many, many of you feel that the personality who you call O. J. should be punished, the plan, the blueprint is that he shall go free or at least not to be condemned to death, and we do this because so many human beings would say, "Justice be served," and then close the door. And they shall no more think on the violence, you call it domestic violence? We call it violence. You see, your thinking is changing. The human beings need to go into higher dimensional thinking at this time and what the lesson is, in truth, is that *all* violence shall not be condoned.

And while it is on a world-wide surface, all of the things that are happening world-wide are a part of that lesson, also. But these cases, my friends, are bringing them to your home. They are coming through your heart for was he not one of your heroes? And was she, Polly, not one of your children?

And human beings need very hard lessons indeed in order to effect change. Change has begun, my friends. You're within a three-year period into this change.

You'll have seven more years of radical change. And then you will begin to truly grow the way you should.

J: So out of the Simpson case will come changes, not only in laws, but also in our own personal intolerance. We will not tolerate violence anymore, whether it's with a spouse or anybody else.

M: Indeed. It is a few of the baby steps we have spoken to you about. Human beings do not change very easily. They need to have dramatic trauma. There are many thousands of human beings being killed each day in their own country by weapons that you all condone to a degree because if you did not condone, there would be more of you who would be putting protest against those things you call guns.

But again, this is a lesson in itself that is so brutal and so horrible to imagine that it will be long on the minds of the people. And if this person is allowed to declare insanity or to declare freedom, it'll even be longer on the minds of people, and it will begin to effect change.

And every which way, you are beginning to effect change. It is a long, hard process for you have condoned violence for millions of years.

It is the last bastion of stubbornness. And human beings have looked at death every day. Have you noticed when you have your killings that are by the way, you know, um....

J: Drivebys?

M: Indeed. People become outraged for a few moments and they say, there but for the grace of God goes my family, and then they choose to turn away and walk into their homes. You see what I'm saying? Babies, little children, and old people have been killed. Innocent bystanders of wars against one another. But it does not make much of a difference to the human mind as long as you can hide away.

But when you have a hero and when you have such brutal murders, it's almost beyond comprehension that just an every day man could do it. You see that's another thing we say to you. In the case of Polly Klaas, that indeed was a low mind, a criminal, a career criminal, if you will. And so that is what is expected of him.

But, in the case of this Simpson, he was a hero. He was an every day man. He was someone who was like you and you and you.

J: People could identify with him.

M: Indeed. And at some point the idea comes about that if he could do that in violence, then what are we capable of doing in violence?

And again, if the person goes to prison and is condemned to death, there will be another doorway shutting and you'll have to have an even harder lesson.

J: And there'll be another case that will enrage us enough to make change?

M: But do you understand what we say that if you have someone in your gangs hurt and kill a small child, that is only to be expected. They are, you have an interesting term, low-life.

J: Yeah. But you don't expect something like that coming from O. J. Simpson who was the hero.

M: From a common man. From the good man. From the man that everybody can identify with. From the man who everyone looks up to, including children. Or the man who someone says, "If he can do that, if he can become rich and powerful, so can I." From the man who gives hope to many thousands of your people who have the brown skin. That if he can rise above his situation, then so can I. And in that very fact if he can do all these things, then so can I.

J: So then people have to be introspective and recognize what they, too, are capable of as well and correct that.

M: Indeed. And that is the lesson, my friends. That if the common every day man could be driven to violence such as that, then we must do something about it. And you know so many of your people condemn your media.

J: Yes, television coverage, the media, the newspeople.

M: Yes. But you see, they are part of the grand scheme of things. They are part of the lesson, for if your media could not speak of it, if they could not deal with it with all the speculation and the presentation of the blood and the gory facts, then it would not soon be in people's eyes.

And on top of that, it will help to allow this person to become safe, and then you will see outrage.

We are so sorry that human beings have to learn this way. But until you no longer need polarities, you shall learn this way. Again, we say to you that most of your institutions will topple, and they need to be rebuilt by the every day man and woman.

J: Right. Including the justice system. What is O. J. personally learning from all this? What's his personal lesson?

M: As a human being, this person needs to learn to let go. He holds on to everything that is near and dear to him. That does seem like a simple lesson, does it not? But in reality, it is very hard indeed. Almost no human being can do this thoroughly.

J: How will his children be affected by all this?

M: They are very traumatized, and they will grow up traumatized.

J: Well, I hope the angels can surround Nicole and Ron with all kinds of good thoughts and light and love from us because we're all thinking of them.

M: There are 2,200 souls who are now in that process. But you see, if human beings learned a little easier, it would not have to have such a trauma. As in your wars, your killings, and your failures of all institutions. You would not have to have such trauma if you chose to learn in a simpler fashion.

Rosie said later that the incident involving Susan Smith, the young mother who rolled her car into a lake with her two sons trapped inside, was the other incident that Miriam mentioned we would be outraged about.

Homosexuality

Another major attitude adjustment is called for with regard to our judgment of homosexuality.

I: There is a great judgment upon your earth this day. Anyone who is different, anyone who does not fit into your so-called word, normal, is looked down upon, has had many negative experiences because of that difference, and needs to be here for a reason. You need to see that because one is different does not mean one is wrong.

That's another major lesson for human beings. You cannot go on if you all have to be similar. It is judgment, and to go on into dimensional thinking that you're striving for at this time, you need to stop with the judgment.

J: Right. We have a real problem, especially in the United States, about judging homosexuality probably because we don't understand it or what causes it.

I: It's not that you don't understand it and what causes it, it's that you fear it. You fear differences, my friend. As a human being, they fear differences.

If they cannot put it into a little box, then it must be different. And if it's different, it's not like them. And so they fear it. Anything of the unknown human beings tend to fear. Anything that cannot be explained, human beings tend to fear. They go through the universe with night lights. Because they must see each and every thing to explain it to themselves. And when they cannot do so, there is a fear. And when there is a fear, there is a judgment, and usually a negative judgment.

Homosexuals are again those souls who came back too fast, who remember other lifetimes, a male who remembers a female lifetime and wishes for it.

It is also because when those souls come back so fast, there is a body memory and a residue of that other time. And so it is very confusing to them. They feel as if they are not the people that they are now. That is one reason why you have homosexuality. It is not something that is often brought about by earth living. It is something that has happened before you come to your earth.

Killers

The subject of serial killers, like Jeffrey Dahmer, came up with reference to what tendencies or signs their parents could have looked for which would have indicated potential trouble and what causes people to become serial killers. Safar had an insightful response.

S: Have you not noticed that in the last twenty of your years, twenty-five in fact, there has been a greater increase in the incidents of these type of people? Do you realize that all of the substances that you put into your earth and into your animals all are negative to the human body for the most part? The pollution you have in the air is negative to the human body, and almost always you'll begin to realize that, from birth on, there are some humans who are so sensitive and have such imbalance in their bodies that things can manifest and destroy their brain cells.

And that has a lot to do with these folks. Another factor is that parents or guides truly do not take the time to guide. But we cannot blame those souls you call parents for all of it.

There are some who come in to bring a message, a universal message, that you have to begin to say no. You have to begin to resist negativity if your world is ever going to go into a higher consciousness of thinking. At one time there were wonderful families who served to be a role model for your public. There came a time when that no longer sufficed, when greed took over and your people decided they needed more. When they received more, they needed more. And so the family broke up.

Another factor is that you did not give your females more of what they truly needed: rights, equality. We find this hard that we are saying this, for in our land we did not do so, either. But then again the little ones and the mothers were kept well out of harm's way.

But, at this time, your females needed to have more say, and if that had been done, then there would not have been a revolution in that sex. And it has been for many eons of time the mother who has made the child.

But this little one that you call Jeffrey started out to be unique, unusual, cruel, and he should have been taken care of. This is also a person who has felt rejected and alone for so long, and he felt truly that he needed to feel once again and so by eating of others, by hurting of others, he began to feel for a short time different emotions. That is indeed the truth. But it never lasted.

Now we say to you, give your little ones boundaries, lots of physical touching in pleasant ways, hugging, touching, choices, and always allow them to gather with you.

Give them joy. Allow them to laugh. Have them laugh with you. And give them strong boundaries. Your children at this time are losing the knowledge of right and wrong. And it is because no one has the time to teach them. They let your picture boxes do the training.

J: True. Or they expect teachers to do it.

S: And then when the teachers try to do this, do not the parents rail against it? "You are taking my place. You have no right." And so until mothers and fathers decide to take over the responsibility of teaching boundaries, of love, gentleness, togetherness, and families, it will get worse. And even though you have such marvelous inventions (televisions), we would throw them out of the house until they can become more productive, more positive, and they can begin to let go of all that you call violence.

In our time we may have been called savages by you who are in this evolution, but we did not have so much cruelty on such a high level.

Michael Jackson

Many popular personalities have faced their own lessons under public scrutiny, none more so than Michael Jackson, an entertainer who certainly has made more than his share of headlines in the last couple of years. We have a lot to learn from him.

I: His teaching, not lesson, but his *teaching* is that power left uncontrolled can be detrimental to all.

J: Right. So people tuning in to Michael Jackson can see that for themselves.

I: They can see a very good soul who has lovingly committed himself to many people, but who has uncontrollable power and does not know what to do with it. There is a tendency for him to want to be like a child. And there is a tendency to want to commune in childlike ways on every level. It is because he is trying to heal and to raise up the child that he still is.

J: Yes, he's a wounded child.

I: Indeed, he has never grown past a certain age level and that being approximately seven to eight years of age. He is beginning to experience sexualness at an age where most of you have already identified what it is and have experienced it at a great deal.

But this child-like personality moves very slowly in his growth. There are parts of this personality, the aspects of the intellect, which can become very adult very quickly, but for the most part, this is still a child.

J: Will he ever mature out of that stage?

I: No, he will not because he will not be with you for a long period of time.

J: Will he take his own life?

I: He has tried once and may try very soon again. We hope not. You see also the aspect of a child is the fear of punishment. And this is power out of control. We do say to you that he has so much more to give than most others of his kind or his persuasion. He has a great deal of love to give to humanity, and it would be a crime for him to end that progression, but we do not see that he shall be with you for a long period of time.

J: Do you know how much longer?

I: From today until approximately five years. Any time in that period there may be a tendency to want to leave. Indeed, there is a desire to leave now. Fear is stopping it. And that is one of us.

J: One of you is stopping him?

I: We are injecting the fear.

J: Well, that's good. Keep it up. We want to have him around. He's a talented, loving being.

I: There is much more to this personality than meets the eye. Again, it is both positive and negative in the philosophies. This is a child who is trying to grow up and has no one there to guide him.

J: But, if he turned to a guide, couldn't he get some help?

I: In his philosophy there's a fear of guides as they are considered adults.

J: Oh, okay. He doesn't trust anybody.

I: Indeed. And as adults, they have the power to punish. Even guides on our side have the power to punish. In his philosophy, guides are God. Many of those souls who wish to help him in his employ, in fact, do not do so out of fear of losing their employment, their way of living, and they have been, indeed, paid very well. And so they choose not to speak to this soul about his actions.

J: So he remains unchecked.

I: Indeed.

J: Why did he marry Lisa Marie Presley?

I: It is a refuge. You have two people who have been damaged. You have two people who are not in the normal range of humanity. They are different and everyone needs a refuge. They have found it in each other.

Donald (Didn't) Trump

Even though angels will help us with any request we make of them, they do warn us to be careful what we ask for. Often we'll ask for something which we don't want once we get it, a very hard lesson, indeed.

I: Some humans think that riches will solve all of their problems, and when they receive winnings or riches, they begin to find out that this is not what would make them happy at all, and they end up more unhappy.

J: Because that's not where happiness lies.

I: For some individuals, it does. But some individuals have very little thought process.

J: Donald Trump has very little thought process?

I: Your Donald Trump's greatest desire in this lifetime is to be accepted. It has nothing to do with riches.

J: Be accepted by whom?

I: By every human being, by anyone. He is like a small child trying for attention. Look, I wrote a beautiful poem. Look, I built a beautiful tower. Look, I got an "A" on my report card. Look, I am rich. Is there not a similarity? This is a personality who's never felt that he has been loved and wishes to be loved, and his way of doing it is to be rich and to be someone. If he could not get publicity and attention, then he would subject himself to diseases.

J: He'd get attention that way?

I: Indeed, he would. He has never felt special, in truth.

J: Still? After all he's accomplished?

I: Still. He has accomplished nothing, my friend. If he had felt that he had accomplished all that he could, then he wouldn't still be needing that attention. It's a sad thing that we see. You see, he has never lost the little boy inside himself that says I am not worthy. It is a sad thing to look upon. It is sad because he has not learned the lesson. He will have to accomplish it some other way.

Stephen King

The "king of scare," popular writer Stephen King, became the topic of conversation when Rosie mixed him up with a discussion of Steven Spielberg. But it was insightful, probing into what makes him so popular and why he writes about such fearful things.

I: Number one, he has a great many fears himself and this is a way for him to let go of his fears. It is as if he has a bogey man under his bed each night, and he is trying to do psychological work on himself and allowing himself to let go of those fears of his childhood.

This is also a personality who enjoys being frightened. He enjoys "roller coaster rides." Those things that scare him give him a rush of a chemical you call adrenalin. We also say to you this personality enjoys making money.

J: (laughs) He makes quite a bit of it.

I: Now we ask you why a personality would deal with so much negative. Can you guess?

J: Because there's a fascination with it, I think.

I: Indeed, because human beings tend to find it easier to deal with the negative than they do with the positive. To deal with the positive is not so exciting, not such a rush.

Human beings throughout your entire history have dealt much better with the negative than with the positive. When you deal with the negative, you say to yourself, "Aw, I knew this would happen." In that way, you can understand your own life. But when you are successful and have many positive things going for you, there is a tendency to be very fearful because maybe at some point the positivity will stop.

And it is not such a bad thing to have a negative thing happen because you can always hope for the better. But when you have the better, there is no way but down in some people's minds.

And so it is not quite so much fun to be positive. Positivity and trying to deal with positivity most of your life is much like eating vegetables. You understand that they are good for you and taste good, but how many times do you cook them?

It is the same with positivity. It is a good thing, it feels good, but how many of you choose to work on positivity all the time? Again, the biggest problem with positivity is the fear that you will lose it. Human beings deal so much better with negativity. There's no way but up with negativity. It is something they understand.

J: Is that why some people like horror movies? Because they can get into that whole thing?

I: Indeed, and they feel comfortable there. It is as if: "I know this. I know what it feels like. I know that adrenalin rush, and so I feel comfortable in this."

It is much more frightening to be in a positive vein. How many of your people enjoy the idea of a surprise party?

J: Oh, most people do.

I: Very few. We disagree with you.

J: Really? Well, I like it.

I: You are somewhat of, let us say, an abnormal person.

J: (laughs) That's true.

I: We would say 90% of your people do not enjoy something for them that is unplanned. They do not enjoy it, even if it is wonderful, nice and beautiful. They'd much rather enjoy the idea that everyone forgot their birthday.

Another thing, when someone gives you a surprise party, it is an honor of yourself, is it not? Ninety percent of your human beings do not feel like honoring themselves, and they feel that it is not a process that can be true for themselves.

J: They don't feel worthy.

I: Indeed. But again, if you have many positive thoughts, actions, and happenings in your life, maybe at some point in the human's life he or she will get to enjoy it. Remember what we have said: it is much easier to be negative because there is no way but up. It is much harder to be positive because there's the fear of positivity leaving, escaping. But you must learn how to do it, my friends, because it is a part of where you are going.

Bill Clinton

Even though he holds the highest elected office in our nation, the president does not rate a special angel for his guidance, but looks to his regular guardian, like all of us.

I: Your president is a personality who does not know which way to turn, and so he is looking under all kinds of bushels, let us say that, in order to have information to help him guide your country. This is a very unsure personality. He is someone that is not aware of his own power and continually is frustrated because he cannot see it. And so he will look all around him. The interesting thing about this human is that he expects so much from others, and yet he does wish to receive all that he feels he deserves.

J: How's the scandal going to turn out with President Clinton and Paula Jones? She's the one who accused him of sexual harassment when he was governor of Arkansas, and now he's counter-suing her, saying she can't interfere with his duties while he's in office.

M: We say to you that the American public is fed up with all the shenanigans that go on with these two. It will eventually be thrown out, unless it is to be used as a catalyst for his downfall. We do not think so at this time.

But the president shall not gain another term. Not at this time. The American public has been fooled once too many times, and he is an ineffectual president.

J: Well, his health care reform appears to be going down the drain.

M: It shall be.

J: It's not gonna be salvaged at all?

M: No, indeed, it will not, and if it is salvaged at all, it will be very shallow. And that, my friend, is a shame.

J: It is. Will we have any kind of reform in terms of health?

M: Eventually, yes. It will take approximately fifteen of your years. There will be little strides made, but not the big important picture that your president saw.

J: Is it because people don't have faith in his abilities?

M: It is because your people on the earth have so much apathy that they chose to allow others to take their votes and to throw them away and to invite in those politicians who choose to think nothing except of themselves.

And when the people become less apathetic, then you shall see true service and that is beginning to happen.

Lefties Are Listening

In some of the New Age publications, there is a growing interest in "sacred geometry," which basically maintains that

—260—

certain mathematical shapes, like tetrahedrons, denote spirituality. This new focus has captured the attention of left-brain souls who are beginning to understand that there's much more to earth than what they originally thought.

I: The right-brain souls have had many evidences of philosophies, of our world, but it is usually in a vision of the spirit. These figures that you have been hearing about is a way for other souls, those who are left-brain dominant, who do not understand visions, as such, to come in and to explain philosophies.

Many of these geometric figures are a way of helping those souls come to terms with themselves and their own philosophies. It's another way of saying that you need to expand your thought processes and energies. And human beings, no matter left, or right, or both, need visions of some sort in order to make them wonder.

And when they begin to wonder about a vision, they begin to think in thoughts and philosophies that they have not thought in before. And so every single thing that is happening on this earth today is for the purpose of allowing people to expand. We ask you something. Why do you think that there are so many people who have a sudden attraction towards angels? Do you think we were not always here?

J: No, I know you were always here.

I: But again, we have come into our popularity, have we not?

J: Very much so.

I: So we say to you that, when those persons choose to expand and to allow our auras, our colors, light, and energy, whatever you wish to call it, then we do so on the double.

And so "sacred geometry" is just to say to many people: there is more than what you have thought. There is more than what you can comprehend at this time. Why not come in and think about it a while?

J: Yeah. It's for the left-brain people to see almost a metaphor for mystery.

I: Indeed.

J: And so they look at this and realize, hmmm, there's a lot I don't understand about the world. Let me investigate.

I: And, indeed, if these left-brain people were to see an angel or a spaceship, do you think that they would believe that they had seen something? They would say that they had been ingesting too many pollutants.

But they can understand these formations, and it gives them pause, and they begin to think that there might be more to life than just their little universe.

One more thought on your geometric figures. We need to tell you that there are certain souls that you call extra-terrestrials who choose to come in and define themselves in that way, also. And that is appealing, again, to the left-brain figure as a way of helping to identify those souls.

J: You lost me on that one.

I: We say to you that, rather than coming in as a little green man...

J: They come in as a geometric shape?

I: Yes.

J: Like a building?

I: Indeed. But they are not a building. You have had some in your group at times where there have been geometric figures in the air.

J: Some of the people in our group have drawn geometric figures.

I: And some in your group have seen them. It is a form of life that chooses to identify themselves in this way. Basically because they are of a higher intelligence, and you would call them also left-brain.

J: I know in one of his books Lazaris wrote about going into another dimension where it was a geometric plane, so is that what he's talking about?

I: Indeed. There are souls like that. And so your figures are two-fold. It is interesting that when you see those entities that you call extraterrestrials, they are not so bright as those other figures. And so that is how you tell the difference.

J: Is that why, then, some people really relate to the geometric design and figures because they see that other dimension in that figure?

I: Indeed. And some see old friends in those figures. We say to you that not all humans were always human.

J: So there's a recognition factor.

I: Indeed. So it is a two-fold purpose. Is that not interesting that nothing is wasted, and you can use it for two different things?

Chapter 9

An Attitude Adjustment

We welcome the idea that so many of you are beginning to speak out your thought processes and to wake up from the apathy that you have experienced.

Institutions Falling Down

E very way of life that we know in this country today will be changing. The education system is at a stand still. The medical system is no longer meeting our needs. The financial system is filled with greed. And our judicial system cries out for massive reform.

I: Many of these systems will be breaking down in the next few years, and there will be a need to build a new foundation for better systems. And those people who are beginning at this time to feel the need to be of service in a certain way, as you do as a teacher, will be in the background in order to pick up the pieces.

J: Sounds exciting.

I: It is exciting. You see, on our side, it is neither good nor bad; it is growth. And so we see the light around all these institutions because we see the growth of those souls who will shine in those institutions.

J: You see into the future?

I: Indeed. The future has great upheaval, but if enough of you souls begin to change, you can change the course of your history and your destiny. If one or two or a hundred speak out or a thousand or two thousand and say to those in power: "We do not believe in this system. We need to change," then enough of you who speak out will be able to change your systems. What would you like to ask about your future?

J: Well, when you were talking about systems changing, I was thinking maybe it was the physical earth. We hear so much about earthquakes and upheaval in that way.

I: That shall always be.

J: Yeah, but it's systems you're talking about.

I: We're talking about the functions of your society. We're talking about your medical system, for instance. It has gone about as far as it can go with all the greed that is accompanying it. There is very little service-related humanity in that system. It is more for the greed of those who operate it.

And until that system falls down, and it shall, then things will not change. We ask you how you feel about taking alternative medicines. Those of you who are beginning to grow at a very fast pace are beginning to see that things are not as they really seem. Your medical system is not as grand as everyone hoped it would be.

J: There are better ways, so we just have to be open to those to change things.

I: And it takes but one. If you decide one fine day that you do not need an aspirin for your headache, but tend to smell some beautiful perfume instead, is it not changed? And so on and so on. That is what will happen. Already there is a fear in this system itself that many human beings are turning away from their organized thinking.

It is the same with the educational system. You will see a great outbreak of crying about this system and the children of this system. And things will begin to change because it will change from the inside out. Human beings will be dissatisfied, and they will begin to change the face of that system.

The New Foundations

We are now into the fourth year of a cycle which will see the tearing down of our educational, medical, monetary, and judicial institutions. In about six years, we will see these institutions re-established, but on new foundations.

I: The more people try to ignore these things in their lives, the more it will falter. You need to begin to speak out, each and every one for yourselves, about what it is that bothers you about all these institutions. You should speak your feelings. Your government, your people in power, will not allow anything to change unless more and more of you speak out.

This is a revolution in your country and it has to be. In order to rebuild the foundations in a positive manner, everything must come down. It is as if the wood of your buildings is rotten from the inside out, and you need to begin to speak on this, to think on this, and to make your feelings known.

The little girl that created such interest in your entire country a few months ago...her name was Polly?

J: Oh, Polly Klaas.

I: Yes, she was the beginning of a cycle to begin to speak out, to begin to start to build a new foundation. Now there have been many children who have been hurt, maimed and murdered in this world of yours, but she was special in that she was the beginning. Indeed, that was her focus for this lifetime. She was the beginning of a movement that said, "No more; we do not wish to put up with this justice, as you call it, anymore."

There is a great deal of apathy in your country at this time. There is a feeling of what can I do? I am but one. Again, if you are a drop of water, and your country is the bucket, if enough of you put your drops into the bucket, it shall overflow.

And so we welcome the idea that many of you are speaking out, and again it will happen at least three more times that you will become outraged as citizens of your country, that things like this could happen in your country. And this will be the beginning of tearing down the rotten foundation and beginning anew.

So welcome this, my friends. It has been planned, and it has been long sought after on our side. Again, all the other institutions will go through much the same. Your medical institution even now is becoming criticized for its methods and the way it deals with human beings. You see, sad to say, most of those souls who deal with human beings in a medical level at this time do not think of them as human beings, but as slabs of meat.

We welcome the idea that so many of you are beginning to speak out your thought processes and to wake up from the apathy that you have experienced. Indeed, we would say three-fourths of your country is apathetic towards anything that is being done. If it does not happen and happen soon, then the entire system will fall apart.

J: Why is it that we feel so disempowered, that we have been silent for so long about so many injustices?

I: Because people tend to think of themselves as the one. They tend to think of themselves as being small and incapable of change for the bigger picture. They think of themselves as not being much help to the bigger picture. There is a greater reason for this that most human beings do not think about, and we would like to speak on that. The reason most people keep quiet about things that they choose to feel offended or angry by is because they do not want to make problems for themselves. They do not wish to be singled out as someone different or a trouble-maker. There is a great fear of what can happen if he or she speaks out.

And so this attitude must change. If there is ever to be the good in this world, it must change. But what it boils down to is self, fear for self and fear for family. Most of you speak about being independent and individualistic, and we would say 99% of you people choose to conform to what everyone else is thinking, doing, feeling because you do not want to be singled out as being different. Well, there are a great number of you who are being born approximately in the last 25 years who *are* different, and there is no way that you can help that. So, you should get to work on your projects. The purpose is to *be* different.

The Plan for Earth

There will be a time when we will have evolved enough as a people and a planet that to be different will be something to be proud of.

J: If the world is expanding, and we're expanding with it, becoming a new civilization. What will we look like 5,000 years from now?

I: The plan for this earth is to become very much like our side, energy beings.

J: So, we'll be light bodies.

I: Indeed. There will be a finding approximately twelve years from now your time, when the structure of the human body will become more uniform.

J: I'm not sure I understand that.

I: We will say to you that some of you are too thin in your mind, and some of you are too fat in your mind, and some of you have problems with different parts of your body. And we dare say to you that we have not met a single human being who is at least satisfied with the body. But, in the next twelve years, there will be a capsule to help the human race become more uniform.

J: Oh, like one size.

I: Indeed. And there will be a great outcry about this in the future after this happens for a few years because there will be a tendency for you all to want more individuality. So, this is a wonderful lesson in progress. It means that so many of you wish to conform at this time, but in the next twenty years, there will be a tendency not to want to conform to everything.

J: Right. We don't want to be stamped out like cookie cutters.

I: But, you see, in reality human beings do. Especially if you as a woman had the most beautiful blonde or brown thick hair and had a slim-lined figure of a breast size that was not too big and not too small, and a small waist and ample hips. That is wanting to conform to almost all of your human standards. Most human beings would like to have a cookie cutter stamp on them, especially if it is pleasing to the eye.

J: But we can't have a thousand Cindy Crawfords walking around, I guess.

I: Oh, but you can and you will eventually do so. Then you will have a backlash of those individuals who choose to say, " I do not want to be a Cindy Crawford" and that is where real progress will begin for the human race.

J: Then we can just start loving ourselves for whatever way we look.

I: Indeed. But, it is interesting that so many of your ideas and philosophies in your world are just words. They do not have the belief system down. They do not have them in the heart. They have them in the mind. And your archangel, Gabriel, says that—and we agree with him by the way—that you need to be working on the heart of the matter, not the mind.

Foundations of Light

While we are rebuilding the foundations of our new institutions for a more enlightened civilization, the angels suggested that we try to build a foundation of light.

J: How do we do that?

I: How do you see the light at this time? How do you program protection into your mind? How do you ask for help from your guides? You must look at a foundation, and you must build upon that foundation one of light, not of negativity, which is more solid than one of light.

Building foundations is not building new brick buildings. It is an idea, my friend. You see, all your foundations, your monetary foundation, your educational foundation, your medical foundation, your judicial foundation, they are not in reality brick buildings. They are thought processes. And there is a need to have you build that thought process with the light.

Most of your people at this time think that a foundation means bricks. It does not. It means to think in the highest form, to do the good for all, and not to think about the greed, and about what is in it for individuals.

And so at a time period coming, approximately within five-and-a-half to six years, this will need to be done. If this is not done, then you souls who are of the light will leave this plane for another level of your planet, and those souls who choose to stay on this—what you call solid—level of your planet will have a great deal of chaos to deal with.

J: Take, for example, the judicial system. The big movement now, at least in the United States, is three strikes and you're out. That's three felonies and you're stuck in prison forever. We've got to look at that whole system, and how we deal with judging people and punishment and take a whole new approach to it, right?

I: Indeed you do.

J: Because I don't think that's gonna work. That's not an answer.

I: It will not. When you have violence, say you have a huge room full of violent people, it will breed more violence. There are many souls who need to start at the beginning with these little ones who have violent natures. At some point, though, human beings need to be responsible for their own light, and if they show a darkness, it is important that they know that they need to respond to their darkness.

Now we do not say that these souls should go free and be allowed to create havoc with others' lives, but we do say that there must be a place where humanity can turn and ignore those souls until there is a reaching out of those souls.

J: But how can you ignore them when they're trespassing and transgressing against people?

I: If you could find a place for these souls to exist on, let us say with water all around it, and you could give these souls the freedom to be in a new life, give them tools and food, and let them make their own culture, you might be very surprised at how it turns out.

J: That would be a grand experiment.

I: And until one chooses to ignore the other, it is a form of consequences. We do not say that you should let these souls roam free amongst all the people that they could cause chaos with. We are saying that the souls need a helping hand, and then you need to back off until the time they reach out, you understand?

And one of two things shall happen. They will become better equipped to survive, they will begin to want to be human beings, or they will annihilate themselves. And either is their choice.

And we will tell you that these three strikes and you're out will not work. At some point, the whole system will fall down around your ears, and you will have to come up with something very specific. You need to understand that nothing shall work until all are committed. But we definitely say that human beings who come in to cause chaos in others' lives come in for a purpose of control. And so they need to learn the balance of control, which means that they need to be controlled in some form. But these people are learning balance in one lifetime. You see, that is very unusual in that most people in the past learn either the positive or negative of control, and then will experience another lifetime where they learn the opposite. These souls who are coming in now, your so-called criminal element, are needing to learn it all at once.

J: But, what about in the case where you've got people who, let's say, were responsible for someone's death, then he or she goes to the other side, he or she reviews his or her life, but he or she is in total denial about that responsibility. How is he or she going to learn from that lesson if he or she doesn't acknowledge that he or she did anything wrong?

I: On our side, you cannot have total denial if you review your life. There is no way to do this. The only way that souls who come to our side can have denial is that they choose not to follow the light, and in that case they are lost. They cannot look at the life as of yet. Until they choose to follow the light, they cannot look at their lives. There is no such thing as denial on our side once you begin the process of looking at self. You have to. There is no other choice, but up until then there is a choice.

Diminishing the Power of Evil

Humanity experiences the duality of good and evil because it has chosen polarities as a way to learn. But in our emerging civilization, we need to get rid of the idea that there is power in evil. The dark side works for us just as the light side does.

I: Have you ever been out on a beautiful summer night when the stars are out and the moon is out and it's nice and dark? And you feel comfortable and loving? Have you ever let anything come into your mind that might frighten you, a noise of a chipmunk, or something that is rustling, and then the mind becomes frightened? That is where you give the power to the darkness. The same with your evil. Evil exists because human beings give evil power. And again it is in compliance with what human beings need to experience.

J: How can we change that concept, though?

I: Do not give evil power. Do not give the darkness power, and you will see that if you give all your power to the light, things will change. Your scientists have found out something very interesting. Let's say there are two people who walk on a street in the dark at night. One person is thinking about the wonderful day he or she had and has a purpose of getting home and wishes to be happy. And another person has many fears of the night, doesn't know what is out there. He's afraid of any noise. He has led a life where there's a great many fears, and a great many bad things have happened to that what-if type of personality.

Now those souls who choose to go on a negative spree will tend to pick that soul out. And it is because that person is giving power to fear and that fear turns into evil. Being negative for a human being is an easy thing, indeed. But being positive is a great deal of work, my friend. And if you give as much power to the positive as you easily do to the negative, you would find that very few things happen to you. Unless you choose to learn a specific lesson. There are many ways to learn lessons, my friend. You do not always have to go by your guide and your blueprint. You can decide to learn from others.

J: But as a society, we seem to be so filled with fear. We let our fears control us.

I: For humans it is easy to be filled with fear. It is a much harder task to be filled with light and positivity. Let us say you are in grade school, and you start out learning how to count to ten. And then your teacher says to you, you are almost ready to learn how to add. Is there not a great deal of fear? It's like, "My, I might not be able to do it. I might not understand the concept." It is so easy to bring fear into something like that.

Wouldn't it be wonderful if you could train your children to say, "Wonderful. I'm ready." But you see, positivity is a much harder lesson to learn. Negativity is one of the lessons that you would consider young, meaning that it is easy to learn. Positivity is one of the old-soul lessons, and it is much harder to learn. We say to you that your negativity is second grade. Your positivity is college level.

Teachers Re-Taught

As we forge a new way of life for all of humankind, the training of teachers must be revitalized to empower the children and build their self-esteem.

I: The educational system will be falling, and so you might be aware that at some point there must be many light workers who will begin to build a new foundation for that philosophy.

J: We need to praise and encourage students as we teach them to see the positive.

I: A great many of those teachers who do this as a way of education do it absent-mindedly. They do not truly mean that this child has done something well or great. The child feels it and feels like this is an untruth.

J: Insincere.

I: Indeed. And so the child still comes through with the lower self-esteem. And many around them wonder why. It is because it must be sincere. When you give a child praise, you must focus only on that child and speak into the eyes. And you must spend time. So many teachers in this time period have not got a lot of time to spread to each one. So they become absent-minded and say, "Good job, how nice," and then they go on to the next, and so it means very little.

J: They have to be specific and say, "Your handwriting is so clear now" or "You know, you chose just the right verb."

I: But, the most important to do is to focus directly and completely on each child.

J: That's what they need. One-on-one attention.

I: Indeed. But they need to have it sincere. And this is something that is not being taught, and it is something that a lot of teachers who have good intentions feel that they must do; they must give praise; they must give positivity, and yet it is on a very scattered level. And so the child does not really pick up on it. If you are going to praise anyone, you must directly focus on that person with the eyes, with the body, with the entire self. And that way it will really be heard.

J: Yes. See, it's the whole issue of self-esteem. When I was a vice-principal and had students in trouble in my office, the bottom line was always that they had poor self-esteem. And that seems to be the bottom line of all kinds of society's problems including crime, drugs and everything else.

I: *We tell you a secret.* Each and every human being must build up his or her own self-esteem.

J: How do they do that?

I: They begin to see themselves as something other than they have seen themselves. They begin to see a light in themselves, a brightness they never saw before. You can say to a person with low self-esteem until you're blue into the face, "You are a good person," but until people see it for themselves, they cannot build their self-esteem. And it happens by success. It happens by doing something that they feel good about. That is the beginning. But every human being, be it a child, be it an adult, be it in between, must begin to build the self-esteem through self. It is nice to have others help them, but it is basically a self-philosophy.

J: And I think when we get over the idea that we have to judge ourselves as good or bad, that we just can accept ourselves as we are, then our esteem can be built up because we don't have to put ourselves down. You know, a lot of what we say to ourselves lowers our self-esteem.

I: Indeed, it does. But, you must also understand that there are very good reasons for this. Once you learn to be low in self-esteem, then you can learn to be out of low self-esteem. You cannot have the lesson without the scenario of low self-esteem. And those souls who are coming in at this time period, from the last 35 to 40 years, are coming in to teach others about self-esteem. So they need to experience the low end of the lesson.

Let's say you go to a person who weighs 300 pounds and works in a dress shop. And she comes up to tell you that you would look very well in a certain dress. Is there a tendency to believe it?

J: No, because you tend to think she doesn't know what she's talking about.

I: Because she is not thin. And you are. Again we say this: each and every person has to believe in him- or herself. And he or she has to begin to believe in pulling him- or herself up. And if you have not learned low self-esteem, if you have not gone through it, you cannot possibly help someone with it, and that is why so many of your counselors and psychologists do not have the beginning of an inkling of what their clients are experiencing. Why do you think that so many more of your souls are going to practitioners, are going to psychics, are going to those souls who deal with the high spiritual level? Because they know in reality that those souls have experienced a great deal of what they themselves are going through.

J: They know that these people will have that empathy and compassion because they've been there.

I: Indeed. Many psychics, channelers, metaphysicians, healers are all still there, and so these little souls can identify with them, and they can grow together. You cannot help anyone if you have not experienced a little bit of what that soul has gone through; just as the large lady in the dress shop cannot tell you what is good for you because she cannot experience it at this time. She may have once experienced it, but then again, the fashions are quite different. And so experience as much as you can and be as positive as you can, but help those out that you identify with the most.

Becoming Infinite Beings

Our ingrained perception that we are finite beings has held us back from fully experiencing our multidimensional selves. We need to give up the idea of being finite and solid in our self-descriptions.

I: How many of your souls on your planet would choose to say to you that I am here and I am solid?

J: Most of them would.

I: But, it is not so. It is an illusion. There are frequencies, there are waves of sound, there are waves of light going straight through your body at all times. And so you cannot possibly be solid, can you?

And so when you begin to think in terms of infinite, you'll begin to really grow, my friend, just as you do in your spiritual growth when you begin to think in terms of infinity instead of only a small part.
You can grow with power. When you begin to think in terms of infinite power, then you can truly grow. And

when you think in those terms, you must begin to believe in those terms. You can think in those terms, but if you do not believe in those terms, then it will not be.

Chapter 10

The Face of the Future

We need to tell you that the world will always
go on. It may not have as many people in it,
indeed, but it will always be, for as long as
you need this schooling.

The Year 2000

L ately there have been television shows speculating about ancient prophecies for the year 2000. But it seems that at every turn of the century, we project fearful, negative events for the future. Although Isabelle sees chaos and upheaval up ahead, there will not be an Armageddon on our pathway by the year 2000.

I: Armageddon is something in the minds of the people as is death, as is heaven, as is richness—all are philosophies. Christianity is a philosophy. It's what you make of it. The same as Armageddon. It is a philosophy. It is what you make of it.

With any of those psychics, seers, or sorcerers, there is a tendency for them to make these prophecies and then for average human beings to give the energy to those philosophies.

And so if you choose to believe in Armageddon, then for many of you that is what it shall be. If you choose to see a bright new world where everyone can begin to love another and have better self-esteem, where greed is not the calling of the day, then that's what you will have.

David observed that while we remember the past as sometimes traumatic, we quake with fear thinking of the future.

D: It is because human beings thrive on fear. It is thrilling for human beings to be afraid. It makes them feel alive. They are afraid of the future, but they tend to be fascinated with it because it frightens them.

If a seer told you that in the future you would have no ups and downs, you would never have to worry about anything, you would have enough money, work, everything that you need, do you think you would be very happy with that reading?

J: *I* would (laughs).

D: Indeed, my friend, you would not. It is a very boring concept not to have fears, dreams, or hopes for the future. If all your wants would be taken care of, you would grow very tired of that in approximately six months. In fact, you would not last quite two years because you would have nothing to live for.

J: No challenges.

D: Indeed. No future. No fear. Nothing to look forward to.

Spiritual Leaders

During the next 250 years, our religious philosophies and processes will be changing a great deal. New times, less violent and filled with greed, will demand new spiritual leaders who will reflect the needs of the emerging civilization.

I: When there are human beings, there will be new spiritual leaders. There are times in your histories that you demand a new spiritual leader. It is a time when you feel totally rejected by your God, and so a new spiritual leader comes. And we will say that in the next 250 years, there will be three on your earth plane.

J: Will there be any female leaders?

I: Indeed. There have been many, but most of you do not recognize females. You see, they are supposed to be loving. They are supposed to be mothers. They are supposed to be caring human beings. And so, by and large, they get covered over.

J: Right. So within 250 years there'll be three of them. Wow.

I: Indeed, they will, but again they will be of your human making.

J: But will any of them be in the United States, or will they be in different countries?

I: They will be in different countries as your states do not feel the need at this time for leadership in that avenue.

J: Nostradamus, the Italian prophet born in 1503, predicted that an anti-Christ will start appearing in 1995 and will pose a great danger to us. This person supposedly will be causing more wars, including atomic warfare. Is any of that accurate?

I: *We tell you a secret.* There are three as of right now. And there have been many anti-Christs all throughout your history. Hitler, Mussolini, Napoleon, Genghis Khan, Charlemagne. Even Richard the Lion-Hearted was an anti-Christ to some.

Christ is a by-word for exalted soul; it is also a by-word for God. So when the Crusaders came to the infidel, they were considered anti-God. Thus there have been many anti-Christs.

And there will be many anti-Christs to come. If you start to deal with your philosophies and your thought pro-cesses directly from the heart and not from fear, not from the mind, you will have more of an instance of knowing who is an anti-Christ and who is not.

Your Hitler was a personality who was given much credit for bringing his country out of a depression. And it wasn't with the human heart that he was allowed to become so strong. It was the fear that if someone didn't help to pull them out of depression and financial abyss, they would all perish.

If those souls had thought within their hearts of what he was doing, we guarantee you that he would not have been as strong as he was. But, because human beings dealt with their own fears, they allowed a soul to become an anti-Christ. And that is what you have to look toward.

A New Perspective on God

Of all the information that was given by the Isabelle group, the most shocking news was that what we think of as the Creator is just the beginning and that there is much more behind that Source. A part of the Creator was made by another Creator. It was David who first delivered this amazing message.

D: The Creator is always in expansion, so is the part of It that was made.

J: *Was* there a part that was made?

D: Indeed. By another.

J: A bigger source?

D: Indeed. There has always been a saying that All That Is. Do you think that holds truth? All That Is is expanding. There is energy behind energy behind energy behind energy. And so there is so much more than that which we can explain to you because even we cannot fully see That That Is.

J: What part of the Creator was made by another Creator?

D: Let us ask you a question. Did you just exist in your beginnings? Or did you have a creator, a mother?

J: Yeah, I had a creator.

D: Indeed. It is much like the same thing. The beginning of your God was a creation made by two forces, what you consider a male and female energy. It was energy. But they came together and split into a third.

J: Did something or someone cause them to come together and split into a third?

D: You could use the term nature.

J: Yes. But were the separate parts, the male and the female parts of this force; were they all still one force? Was it one Creator?

D: It is indeed so, but we need to tell you something. Where do you think the idea of balance of energies has come from?

J: From trying to create just like the Creator. I mean, we have been told we're made in the image and likeness of

God, so I would imagine that that's what the image and likeness of God is, male and female principles.

D: Indeed. And that was needed again to bring about your Creator, the balance of male and female energies. It is not like your human male and human female. It is a positive and a negative ion. But again that, too, has been created by a force. And it goes backwards twelve upon twelve upon twelve. Into infinity.

J: Why the number twelve?

D: We do not know this. It is just what has happened. We tell you something interesting. Your Creator has created this earth and your universe. There are other forces who have created other universes and other earths, and they, too, began this way. So we need to tell you that for another universe, you have another God.

J: But who makes that God? How does that God exist?

D: The forces that created your force also created other forces. Let me explain it simply to you. If you take a male and female and they decide to have a child, do they always stop there? Do some of your male and female energies choose to have two, three, four, five children?

J: Right.

D: And it is so with energy.

J: But behind all the multiple energies and the multiple universes, is there just one force?

D: Indeed. It is the great void. It is the absence of all and whole. It is the true balance between all and none. It is the true balance between positive and negative. It is the true balance between male and female energies. It is the all. But you see, it can be the absence of all, and it can be the whole. It is the only thing that you can say is complete. It is the ultimate balance.

D: In approximately ten years you will have a great expansion of what your Creator is.

J: Why is that?

D: Because you will have more chances to deal with our side. It will occur in parts of the mind that have not been used before. Has it not started to happen to you?

J: Yes. There is a leap in consciousness happening.

D: Indeed. A giant leap. Humans are becoming a little more mature in their thinking, actions, and philosophies. Human beings are truly one of the youngest souls in your universe. A great many souls start out in your planet because it provides a quick growth session. It takes much longer in other planetary systems to grow as fast as humans do, but that is the reason why so many younger souls start out on earth.

Your people call an old soul one who's had maybe 50 to 250 lifetimes. But there are many souls who have lived thousands of lifetimes away from your planet. They still consider themselves not old.

J: How many lives have I led?

D: Three hundred and twenty-seven. Not all being of this planet. On this planet, forty-seven.

J: Wow! Getting back to the Source behind the Source, for a moment, Is this chain of command, the God behind our God, is that chain infinite? Is there ultimately one supreme God or does it continue like the earth which has all kinds of dimensions? Does God have all these dimensions, too?

D: Your God is not human, it is not a being. It is a force and it is a light, a feeling, an emotion even, whatever you choose to call it. But it is not a little old man. It is not someone who is sitting upon a chair to throw down rewards or punishment. It is a force, a light. And where there is light, there must be a source to direct that light to have it turn on, if you will.

And we say to you, yes, it is infinite. We can tell you at this time that you would consider it finite because it has not expanded for a short time.

J: I don't understand that last statement.

D: Many of you have time elements. Many planets have time elements, and we say to you that it is not expanding constantly. It rests.

J: It's like inhaling.

D: Indeed.

J: We inhale and we stop, and then exhale and stop.

D: But just as you have a light bulb, does that not give off light? But there is something behind it to make it give out light. More power. Electricity. But where does that electricity come from? From the little socket or is there something behind that?

J: Behind that.

D: It is always power, is it not?

J: So there's a power behind what we understand is God.

D: Indeed. There are powers behind powers behind powers that you could not even imagine. And, indeed, even on this side, it is very hard to imagine. It is so immense. It is continuing. There is no ending.

J: It's infinite.

D: Indeed. But if you wish to have a God who has a great white beard, with bright blue eyes, and someone who says to you, "You have been a bad person," or "You have been a good person," that will be provided.

Now there are a great many of you who would not relish this idea. They choose to enjoy a reality of their philosophies. And we allow that, as everyone should allow everyone's thought processes.

And so if you wish to say that our God is *the* God, the *only* God, and there is nothing after that, this is also of interest to some. But it does not mean that it is all that there is.

I: *And we will tell you another secret.* The human being is a conductor for the experiences of the Creator, which means that you are acting as conductor with all of the lessons that you learn; you are a filter for your Creator to experience different balances. It is an enjoyable process—for your Creator.

J: (laughs) It's not always enjoyable for us.

I: Indeed. But most human beings choose this, you see. That is why your Creator gives you free will because it makes so many different and unique experiences.

J: And that's what the Creator delights in.

I: Indeed. Do you know that we take offense at those who say He or She.

J: Oh, for the Creator?

I: Do you know why? Because the Creator is a balance of male and female energy. And so there is no such thing as just He because you invalidate the other part of the Creator. So we much rather like the idea of the Source. Or the Creator because it implies wholeness and balance.

J: Or if you said It because there's no gender assigned to it.

I: But human beings would not allow themselves to say

that. They have a fear of thunderbolts.

J: (laughs) Somebody's gonna get 'em for saying that.

I: Indeed. You see, in your time period on your earth plane, on our plane, there is no such thing as imbalance. And when you say He or She of the Creator, you are implying that your Source is unbalanced.

J: Oh, how insulting.

I: Indeed.

J: Okay. Well, we'll get the word out it's not politically correct.

I: We expect that you shall do that. Just as we ask you to understand this. You have groups of people on your earth who call themselves African-Americans, Mexican-Americans, Spanish-Americans, Italian-Americans and all those other names. You are implying that you are not balanced when you do this. That you have to be one or the other. If you begin to say, we are Americans, you will imply we are the whole, the all. And that might be an interesting thing to look at at some future date.

J: Yes, I think that's a very valid thing to say.

I: In fact, it would mean a much nicer thing to say to another person, instead of I am a female, you might begin to say, "I am human." Or "I am balance." Or "I am a person...a soul."

One Worldwide Government

During the next fifty years, we will have a council of twelve, comprised of representatives from twelve countries, but governing global activities.

I: And this is how it will start. And that will happen from today until the next 50 years. It started with your World War II. It has become much more advanced in the last few years.

J: What countries will there be involved in this?

I: In the world government, everyone. It will be democratic in that you will choose each council, each place, each seat, every five to ten years depending on what you choose. Each and every government will have a chance to help make decisions.

J: So will the United States, Russia, China and Japan, and all the major countries be involved?

I: Many of those countries will be instrumental in starting the very first council, yes.

J: All right. So that's going to happen in about 50 years?

I: You have already started. The process started soon after your World War II, but it has speeded up, and you have approximately 50 years in which to make this council happen and to begin to use it wisely.

J: And there won't be any more world wars?

I: If you can begin to use this council wisely, that will be so.

As the worldwide governing council takes hold, the good news is that we will begin to see a rise in the popularity of trade through the bartering process. The bad news is that our national debt will still be here.

J: Will we ever get rid of our debt? I think we're in the trillions of dollars right now as a country.

I: No, you will not. And it will be your falling down. Most of your other countries are having this problem, also. Your Russia? They are having to think more about food and about other people's problems than their defense. And that is all because the monetary system in that country is falling down.

J: So we'll be getting more into trading and bartering as this new world government comes to form.

I: Indeed. The more you get into the spiritual side of yourselves, the less you will desire—of anything.

J: And the more harmoniously we'll cooperate with one another, I think.

I: Indeed.

New Plagues

Because the tropical rainforests being cut down and ancient spores have suddenly been released into the atmosphere, we speculated about future viral epidemics. For example, the recent Ebola breakout in Kikwit, Zaire, Africa, may be one. David informed us that at least fifteen of them are coming.

D: You see, when you change the environment of your planet, when you cause the destruction of your planet, you are going to unleash many things that you have not seen before. And it has a great deal to do with pollution and greed. If you wish to create this destruction, your planet will go on and again it will see humans. Humans may all but disappear off the face of the earth, but not totally.

We tell you a secret. Nothing, nothing is written in stone. Not one thing. Everything can change, except unconditional love. It is the one shining thing that humans have to look forward to. And that is from your Creator.

Extraterrestrials

While it may sound shocking for some of us to think that alien beings seeded this planet, there are those who have at least suspected their presence among us—a presence which has been systematically denied by our government officials. In 1994, *Omni* featured a series of articles on a pervasive government cover-up of knowledge of extraterrestrial encounters which Isabelle corroborated.

I: Let us say this to you. You have a writer who wrote a story of Big Brother? And everyone had a great fear of this. We are here to tell you that your big brother is really looking over your shoulder even now. There are many in your government who tend to think they know what is best for the child. Everyone else being the child. This is a control issue, and it is a power issue. And we say to you that there is a *huge* cover-up, more than you could ever realize.

J: Yeah, I had a friend who worked in Guam years ago and handled big radar machinery, and he knew that there were UFOs, and yet he was sworn to secrecy.

I: There are some who have been threatened with death, and there are some who have disappeared because they spoke of these things. There are some souls in your government who choose to have power above anything else, so when that power is threatened, then the personality who threatens that power must be dealt with and in a very fast, cold way.

There are many evidences of crashes, and use of technology was advanced faster than normal because there are tools and machinery that have been found and that are even now being analyzed and played with. And that is one reason why many of these souls do not wish to talk about this because they wish to have control over other countries. They wish to have power that is greater than anyone else's. And so they do this in an underhanded way. They convince themselves that any human who knows about this should forfeit life as a way of protecting the country.

You see, this is all something that they convince themselves to do, but it boils down to use of power and control and wishing to have even more power. That is the problem with your power in your world. Many souls do not feel as if they get enough, and when they get power, they tend to feel that it is still not enough, so they continue to ask for it, and it's a very narcotic-like feeling.

J: So, aren't we ready now to know the truth?

I: There are a great many of you ready for this, we say that. But are those who are in control ready to give up their power? And that is why things have not moved forward. No matter how much the people are ready to hear this news and welcome it as evidence of existing among others, there are those in power who love to share their power and knowledge with no one. And that is who is controlling your destinies at this time.

Within the next fifty years a new planet will be discovered in our universe, and within a few short years communication with extraterrestrials will be a common occurrence. It will be interesting to see how our government handles this phenomenon when they have spent years covering up our contact with alien life forms.

I: Indeed, there are many planets who have great capabilities, great intellect, and yes, there will be communication eventually. This has been planned for the last three years to make contact with more and more souls. Unfortunately, there is a tendency for humans to become very afraid of these things. Why do you think that most of your movies have come about in a way where there is compassion and gentleness from those souls from other places?

J: Like *E.T.*?

I: Indeed. You see, there must be a training session. There must be education, and the way humans seem to get education these days is through your viewing processes (TV). And so there is much nudging on this side, and on other planes that are somewhat like this side, to be able to help the process along.

J: Right. So Steven Spielberg is doing the world a huge favor in developing movies that will give us a softer picture of extraterrestrials so that we won't be afraid.

I: *We will tell you another secret, my friend.* That is because your Steven is not human.

J: He isn't? Is he extraterrestrial?

I: Indeed, he is.

J: Where's he from originally?

I: Anteres.

J: Does he know this?

I: No, he does not. He chooses to think of himself as very talented in the imagination. And this is indeed a good way to go because it allows him freedom. There was a movie about light beings. A metamorphosis...you call it *Cocoon*. That is very much like his planet.

J: Oh, how exciting. Will he be doing something like a movie in the future that would bring more about his planet to light?

I: What he will be doing in the future is what he is doing now, my friend. He is bringing about understanding and a way of letting go of fears. He is bringing about knowledge. And that is very important. As he has chosen his last subject, it again is knowledge and letting go of fears. People who feel shame also feel fear.

He came into this planet for the reason of experiencing humanness and to experience both balances, that between alien and human. And so he does need to be human in this experience in order to understand humanness, in order to help let go of fear. He needs to experience a different polarity. Neither positive or negative, but that of opposite.

J: When did he come in, then, as an extraterrestrial?

I: This is the second lifetime.

J: When was his first?

I: That of your second World War. As a small child. Boy. Jewish.

J: He was in the holocaust.

I: Polish.

J: That's why he did the movie, *Schindler's List.*

I: And part of his family that died is part of himself. Being one child that died very early in age.

J: So he came back to bring us this movie which accounts for all that trauma and so that we can learn out of that to be more compassionate with one another.

I: Indeed. *Now we will tell you another secret.* There are many so-called aliens upon your planet, and every single one of them who is working for the betterment of understanding is indeed a light worker. Again, you come in to experience humanness. You have experienced angelicness. And so you have balance in the purpose. He has experienced humanness. He has experienced alien. And he balances that.

J: Are there extraterrestrials who are not working for our good, that are evil, maybe, just trying to pull us under?

I: There are extraterrestrials who are experiencing polarities and, as you do, the positive and the negative. Just as you humans experience positive or negative, so do some of these aliens. There are some aliens who are doing experiments, who do not consider it negative to work on lower species.

J: They consider us lower?

I: Indeed, they do. Do you not consider your animals a lower species? But, in fact, are they? No, they are different. But they do not have all the functions that humans have and so humans tend to look down upon them. And this is what some aliens do. We do not say this is a good thing, but it is the same type of thinking that humans experience with their own species.

J: But what abilities do extraterrestrials have that we don't?

I: They are here, are they not?

J: (laughs) They got here. Yeah.

I: They can command humans to come. They can do experiments with many different tools you have not even thought about. They have a different form of energy. They have a different form of movement. Some of them can change. You have a saying in your world, shapeshifters. Some of these aliens can do just that, my friend. And, in their thinking, be it positive or negative, whatever you choose to think, they tend to think of you as a lower form of species.

We also say to you that in their terminology they have helped you to begin. Let us say, seed your planet. And so for them, there is a tendency to indeed think of you as a lower species.

J: What kind of experiments do they perform?

I: At this time there are a great deal of experiments on the brain, on the human body and the organs. Also, the sexual organs are a great interest to those souls because they have lost theirs.

J: How do they reproduce?

I: There are ways that are clinically taken to take what you call seed from their bodies and to implant it in humans and other species.

J: And they're doing that now?

I: Indeed, they are. There have been some children born to humans who are not fully human.

J: Do they look like the other being at all?

I: Some of them.

J: What do the parents do in that case?

I: They choose to feel that they have a freak of nature. They call these things handicapped.

J: So, a handicapped child could be the result of a union between aliens and humans?

I: Indeed, especially if that child has physical features that are not like human features. Let us say, for instance, no ears or no lips. Or the eyes are elongated. Or the eyes are without lids. Or those children who seem to have scales upon their skin. Most of these differences are physical, but there have been some instances when the human body does not react in the same way or the blood of that child is not the same.

J: And doctors know this?

I: Indeed they do.

J: Why hasn't this all come out?

I: It has in various medical papers. They are beginning to find different types of blood at this time period. It is very well known in some medical circles. They choose to think of it as a phenomenon of mutation.

J: So they really don't know how to account for it.

I: Indeed. In fact there are many little souls who are being born who are different, who come into this life with powers of the mind that are not normal for humans. They tend to deal with mental telepathy and with knowing of things.

J: And this is because they are alien?

I: Let us say, half. Does this surprise you?

J: Well, it sounds almost like "The X Files."

I: Has it not been a long-known fact that your scientists experiment on animals and try to mate them together to have different breeds?

J: Yeah, they do that.

I: And why do you think this is so unusual with those souls who feel that they are experimenting on a lower breed?

J: It's the same thing.

I: Indeed, it is. You might choose to have a play about this and begin your own television series. You might try to write something where a child is half and half and the interesting aspects of that.

J: Yeah. That'd be really interesting.

I: We'd like to ask you a question. You mentioned a few moments ago that this sounded to you like a television plot. Why did you say this?

J: (laughs) The whole thing sounded like science fiction.

I: But why? Because it is not in your reality to think that this process could be? It is almost more than the thought process could handle. The real reason is because humans do not like to believe that they could be a lower species, number one, and could be controlled by any other species, number two. They do not like the idea that they can be termed animals or animalistic. And so, for them, in their minds, they choose not to deal with that thought process. It becomes alien to them and very repugnant as any other process that is not known. And this is why human beings have such a terrible time.

Human beings, for the most part, choose to feel that they are the top of the line and are the most expensive cars in the universe. They do not deal well with the idea that they do not have a huge amount of intelligence compared to others. They like to have each and every thing revolve around them. And when they find out that they are not very high on the list of species, it becomes something that is shameful to them, almost horrendous, that they could be thought of as something less than they feel they are and that is why humans have a great deal of difficulty with species other than themselves.

It seems interesting that most humans tend to have to think that they are better than others or that they are better than their animals, that they are better than their counterparts. And so we find that that is a philosophy that indeed needs to be changed.

J: Yes, it does. We resist the thought that anybody is smarter or has control over us.

I: How many of you choose to feel that you do not want to be in reality different from others of your species? How many of you choose to feel that you do not want to identify with those species of our species who are considered handicapped or retarded? How many of you choose to feel that you must not be different—even in your philosophies? Even with how you deal with others who are considered of a lesser nature? And how much has that feeling delayed your progress?

And we say to you that this is ending, my friend. That is what you're dealing with. And that is why there has been so much more activity with aliens in the last three years. Because you are coming to a point when you can deal with other species and not feel so very much smaller.

J: And the more compassion and acceptance we have of handicapped people or people who are different from us, the more we'll be able to accept the fact that there are beings higher in intelligence than us.

I: Indeed. And, the more that you accept the lower species on your own planet, the more you can accept higher species from other planets. In the early 1950s there was a great fear of the idea that there could be anyone else besides themselves, that they had to be a top of the line. And whenever anything was of an aspect that they didn't understand, they became very frightened and sometimes violent. So you have progressed from that time until this time a great deal, my friend, a great leap forward to the point where you choose to see if you could make friends with extraterrestrials.

J: Yeah, we've come a long way.

I: Indeed, you have.

In talking about our origins and the extraterrestrial connection, Isabelle indicated that our past includes a catastrophe when aliens came crashing into our sea. And, although that particular civilization did not survive, Safar said there are others in our ocean with whom we will establish contact in the not-too-distant future.

S: *We will tell you a secret.* There are many places under your sea that do have civilizations that are alive and are not from your planet. One place being your cold land? Arctic?

J: Under the arctic circle?

S: Indeed.

J: Will we ever find out about them?

S: Oh, yes, you will. What has been planned is within the next four years. But how many of your people would be willing to welcome them? And we say to you that your souls will not be allowed to harm these others.

J: Why would they want to? Out of fear?

S: Indeed. Is that not what human beings work upon?

J: Yeah. So they're going to emerge from underneath the Arctic.

S: And other places.

J: And tell us who they are and how long they've been there?

S: They will tell you as much as you can take in. Do you not understand that you're having people abducted? Do you know why? Some of it is experimentation. Again, indeed, there is a great need for new blood. The two civilizations that were dying out are again beginning to die out.

J: So they're coming to get more people to populate their planet?

S: Indeed.

J: How do our human beings live in their planet when we've got such a delicate combination of....

S: Because you have a part of them within the body. You understand?

J: Not exactly.

S: We say to you that these souls do experimentation with breeding upon your people and their people.

J: So that we can adapt in their environment.

S: Indeed, because you are not whole human.

J: Yeah. So they've been breeding people here to take over there that are ready to adapt to that environment. But against their will.

S: When you were born, did you have a will?

J: Well, we always thought we did.

S: Well, can you remember when you were approximately three months old, did you wish to be human? Neither do these. And because they are not upon your earth, they have nothing to miss.

J: Oh, I know what you're saying. They have nothing to compare. Okay. So we're going to find out all about this. Now, when these spaceships come....

S: Are you not already finding out about it? Have you not had many people come forward all of a sudden? You see, that is part of the plan. They are being allowed to remember. As a means of communication so that many of your people will not fear so much.

And, in fact, until approximately ten years ago, they were not allowed to remember at all, and they did not do so. You see, they are much further advanced than you can imagine. And so, those who do remember have been

—312—

given the ability to remember.

J: I see. Well, what are these other civilizations like? How do they organize their people, govern, and treat each other?

S: Some of them have been warring planets. And that is why the decimation of their people.

J: Do they have nuclear warfare like we do?

S: They have gone past that. Have you ever had a high-pitched energy sound upon the ears? Well, multiply that 100 times.

J: And that's what they do to one another.

S: Uh, sometimes.

J: It shatters things?

S: Everything. You call explosion? We say to you explosion of the material known as the body. The heart, if you have a heart. The lungs, if you have a lung. You know, different things. There have also been planets who have agreed upon numbers of souls to kill in order to keep a tally.

J: You mean, the warring planets keep a tally of how many people are killed?

S: They agree to kill their own because it is much more softer.

J: I don't think that they're that advanced, then, if they're into killing their own.

S: We say to you that this was all long ago. And now you have the evidence of a need to have more human involvement in species.

J: Well, why would they seek us out if we're so inferior?

S: Because you are the cousins.

J: We're the closest to them physically?

S: You are the cousins.

J: Are these the grays that we're talking about?

S: Indeed.

J: The ones that look like silver with the slanted eyes?

S: We ask you a question. How many of your people look like you?

J: A lot.

S: But how many? Everyone?

J: Oh, no. But similar. Nobody looks exactly like me.

S: Indeed. And we say to you that this planet has been visited by over fifty-two of these planets. And each and every one has a difference.

There are some that are quite amazing. They are very tall, and they have these beautiful black eyes that go straight up. Unfortunately, they have no hair, and we do not understand why they do not grow them, but they do not. And so they are very shiny in their body material. And they only have four appendages, you call them, fingers. And they are very long. And at the bottom of these things, they can suck things into them, like the elephant. We find that wonderful. They can do most wonderous things with those appendages.

There are some who are so very tiny. You have souls on the planet that we used to call dwarfs, and you call little ones? We have some who are smaller than your littlest one.

J: Like midgets?

S: Indeed. You have others who are quite hairy, who do appear somewhat ape-like. You have others who appear reptilian. You have some that do not appear in any type of form that you call symbols, you know, your wonderful circles and triangles and squares. That is what they show up in.

You have some who can transform their bodies at will. There are some people or some, we'll call them people at this time, who have learned that they can transform the chemistry, the molecules of the form, into other forms. They've begun to realize that they are not solid. You have some that you call amphibian-like. And this is an interesting specimen to study.

J: And they're here on the planet, too?

S: They do not always stay on your planet. It is not hospitable for many of them. But some come to visit. Some come to observe. Some come to experiment. And some come to capture. You do not have to worry. You are safe.

J: Good. Bud had a question. Why is it that some of the aliens have no sexual organs? Are they not interested in sex?

S: Because they inbred so much, they began to make rules out of no breeding at all.

J: What happened when they inbred?

S: There were many atrocities. And the planet began to die off because those that came after were not allowed to breed.

And yes, they had something that you call nuclear war at times on different planets. And it caused great mutations. So there are many planets who have learned what you are now learning.

And, yes, contact is now even being made. Don't you realize how many of your souls are coming forward and saying: "Yes, I have had that."

J: Yes. In fact, I have a friend who was visited by a gray in Grass Valley, I think, and his story was written about in a book.

S: Do you mean by book, a scroll?

J: Yeah, he wrote his story up, and it's in a book along with other people's accounts. But it did happen to him.

S: Indeed, it did. But we say to you there is purpose behind the telling. There is purpose the being was allowed to remember. And that is because you humans have such a fear capacity that we do not want all-out bloodshed.

So, more and more of you will begin to be allowed to tell your stories. And more and more of you will find that it is not such a frightful thing indeed. And so you will begin to make contact.

J: When we do, will we discover abilities to share experiences with these beings? I mean, will we have a friendly relationship with some of them?

S: Not much knowledge will be given to you in the beginning.

J: Why?

S: Because humans misuse knowledge. They usually use it for their own purposes—almost always greed and power. Look what I have. Look what my province has yours has not. And now I want tribute. Has it not happened throughout time?

You know, we would find it very hard, indeed, to have to deal with fear as much as you people deal with fear. And we say that the time we were here last, we did not have much to do with fear, either. But we were one of the lucky few.

And it is a sad thing to have to look upon a world that is so totally filled with fear and anger. It would be a good thing, indeed, to try to start dealing with kindness and happiness.

Light Workers

To speed up our growth, "light workers," a group of angels who work toward promoting enlightenment, are populating the planet. They have come into our history at this particular time to experience what it's like to be human—to take on the problems and sorrows of humankind in order to help out human society.

Of course, not everyone is able to welcome this great angelic invasion. In fact, some people feel that the strong presence of angels among us as a sign of impending doom. But Isabelle was most reassuring.

I: People feel that because more and more communication is being made towards our plane that there must be some huge catastrophe in the making. We need to tell you that the world will always go on. It may not have as many people in it, indeed, but it will always be, for as long as you need this schooling.

New Colors

Because the microcosm reflects the macrocosm, a new paradigm calls for fresh new colors dominating the times.

M: You will have, if you do not destroy your earth, some of the greatest moments in your history in approximately 50 to 100 years. You will come together, and you will blend into a oneness, and each and every one of you will be individualistic, but when coming together to blend, it will be as individuals. And your thought processes will be very much like ours.

J: The whole planet will be transforming.

M: Yes, by braiding two different and joyful colors and noises and sounds and frequencies and anything else you can imagine. It will be as if you will have harmony in the vibration of the earth.

J: That's exciting.

M: And we are hoping that you do not fall down.

J: Well, so are we.

M: Look for the colors of peach, peach-salmon. The more that happens, the more you are gaining ground.

J: Okay. You mean, around us in the air or just the color becoming more prevalent?

M: Around you in the air, in your earth plane. In your sky.

Parting Messages

Safar: We say to you truly, truly, my friends, live through joy. Denounce fear. Denounce anger. Denounce prejudice. Only then can you begin to understand what life is all about.

Those moments that you have experienced in total joy, reach for them. They are all there. Reach for more. Become greedy upon joy. Become powerful upon joy. And you say it is so hard to be joyful at this time, but it is not. You open your mouth. You begin to laugh.

Practice laughing. Practice touching. Practice joy. And you will begin to change as if overnight. You'll begin to bloom like all the glorious roses that I once had. Each and every one different, but each and every one special. Each and every one with his or her own smile, his or her own fragrance. Smell humanity. It might begin to smell very good indeed.

So find that little seed upon your heart and cultivate it. It is a hard thing to do, joy. It takes great perseverance. It takes much thought. But pretty soon you begin to tell another a joke. You begin to say, "I greet thee in joy." And we say to you that when you do that, you become a beautiful mirror upon which that lesson is written. And others will partake of it. See if it does not happen.

Miriam: And we would like to say one thing to your readers. You must begin, my friends, to love yourselves in a way that is God-like. You need to give yourself one important element that very few of you do at this time.

Now when we say love yourselves, we do not mean that you build a fine house or that you cut your hair at a fine cutter's, or that you give yourself the finest foods, buy yourself the finest clothes. That is not love of self. That is dealing with what other people think of you.

But there is one thing that will prove that you can love yourself and you can love the God within, the one element that most of you are missing in this time period. Give yourselves a bit of time to know yourself, to find out about who you are, to see the good in yourself and do more for yourself in this element of time. That is important.

And give of yourself a little time also to others that you do not know. Do you not realize how very good you feel when you give a bit of time to another? It does not have to be in any grand scheme of things. It can be a little bit of time, a few minutes of your time that is so valuable to all of you. That is how you truly begin to love self.

It has nothing to do with giving self material possessions or of telling self that you are truly a fine person. It has to do with the thing that you most honor in your lives and that is time. And so it needs to be done and very quickly because most of you will be facing much harder times in the future, and if you can give yourself self-love and time, you will not feel them so very strongly. There is change in the wind, my friends, and you need to change and go with that flow. If you do not, then you will have a very hard time indeed.

David: The authenticity of this book will be from the heart of anybody who chooses to read this. We do not wish souls to conform with every single word in this book. We wish souls to think about the information and make up their own minds. And if it feels right in your heart, that is how you find that it is real information. If you do not feel that this information is truth, then it is not so for you. Because information is always changing, each and every person needs to use his or her own discernment.

There are no black and white areas in truth. It is how you perceive truth that is true unto you. And what you perceive as truth at this very moment in time may not be the perception a week from now, a month or year from now. It is always changing.

The only way you can see truth of the unknown is by looking into the heart. You see, there truth cannot be lied about. It cannot be hidden. It is always there. Most of you put up walls so that you cannot even see your own truth from the heart, but it is still there.

And we will tell you a final secret. There is nothing that can stand in the way of the heart. Nothing. All prophecy, all thought processes of what will happen in the future can be changed. All.

And it can be changed by using your own discernment, by speaking your truth, and by using the heart. It cannot be changed by using fear. That is the only way that prophecy can become true—by fear. And you can always stop the negative, always.

Isabelle: We say to you, my friends, with the new message that your Gabriel has given to humanity, to live in peace and joy within yourself while all around you there may be chaos. But if you could open your arms and flow all of the good of your universe back to each and every soul that your vibrations, your nature, your thought processes touch, you will live in joy and peace while all around you may not, for each and every one of you will be a beacon, a light.

Others will want to follow. Others will want to know what it is that you have that they don't. So begin to teach the word "allow." That is the closest you can come to unconditional love.

If you help but one, you have succeeded in your task of being human. It is a task of being a soul and of enlightenment. So help but one, help many, but remember that each and every one that you help, you lighten your own load.

And we say to you that we are always with you. You are never alone in any endeavor. All you but do is need call on one of us, and we will be here in a flash, for we can move much faster than you.

J: (laughs) I know that's true.

I: And again, honor the balance of all. Peace be all.

J: Peace be all.

Index

Notes

The Angels Speak:
Secrets From The Other Side

Name: _____

Address: _____

City/State/Zip Code: _____

Telephone: (day) _____(night) _____

Number of copies: _____x $14.95 per book

Sales Tax: $_____
Please add 7.25% for books shipped to California addresses.

Shipping: $_____
Book Rate: $3.00 for the first book and $1.00 for each additional book
(Surface shipping may take three to four weeks)
Air Mail: $4.00 per book

Total payment: $_____

Payment: ☐ Check ☐ MasterCard ☐ VISA

Card number: _____

Cardholder's name: _____ Exp. date:_____

Call toll free and order now: 1-800-683-4545

Please make check or money order payable to: **Prairie Angel Press**

Mail to:

**Prairie Angel Press
P.O. Box 340815
Sacramento, CA 95834-0815
916-658-8450**

DO YOU HAVE A QUESTION
TO ASK THE ANGELS?

Fill out the form below, printing or typing your question—
and being sure to include your telephone number so we can
verify it's really your question if it is chosen to appear in the
upcoming book:

The Angels Speak: Answers to Your Questions.

Please send to:

Prairie Angel Press
P.O. Box 340815
Sacramento, CA 95834-0815

— — — — — — — — — — — — — — — — — — — —

Question: _____

_____

_____

_____

_____

Name_____

Address _____

City/State/Zip Code_____

Telephone (day)_____ (night)_____